Cambridge Elements

Elements in the Philosophy of Mathematics
edited by
Penelope Rush
University of Tasmania
Stewart Shapiro
The Ohio State University

MEDIEVAL FINITISM

Mohammad Saleh Zarepour
The University of Manchester

CAMBRIDGE
UNIVERSITY PRESS

CAMBRIDGE
UNIVERSITY PRESS

Shaftesbury Road, Cambridge CB2 8EA, United Kingdom

One Liberty Plaza, 20th Floor, New York, NY 10006, USA

477 Williamstown Road, Port Melbourne, VIC 3207, Australia

314–321, 3rd Floor, Plot 3, Splendor Forum, Jasola District Centre, New Delhi – 110025, India

103 Penang Road, #05–06/07, Visioncrest Commercial, Singapore 238467

Cambridge University Press is part of Cambridge University Press & Assessment, a department of the University of Cambridge.

We share the University's mission to contribute to society through the pursuit of education, learning and research at the highest international levels of excellence.

www.cambridge.org
Information on this title: www.cambridge.org/9781009618434

DOI: 10.1017/9781009047623

When citing this work, please include a reference to the DOI 10.1017/9781009047623

First published 2024

A catalogue record for this publication is available from the British Library

ISBN 978-1-009-61843-4 Hardback
ISBN 978-1-009-04850-7 Paperback
ISSN 2399-2883 (online)
ISSN 2514-3808 (print)

Medieval Finitism

Elements in the Philosophy of Mathematics

DOI: 10.1017/9781009047623
First published online: November 2024

Mohammad Saleh Zarepour
The University of Manchester

Author for correspondence: Mohammad Saleh Zarepour,
mohammadsaleh.zarepour@manchester.ac.uk

Abstract: Discussing various versions of two medieval arguments for the impossibility of infinity, this Element sheds light on early stages of the evolution of the notion of INFINITIES OF DIFFERENT SIZES. The first argument is called 'the Equality Argument' and relies on the premise that all infinities are equal. The second argument is called 'the Mapping Argument' and relies on the assumption that if one thing is mapped/ superposed upon another thing and neither exceeds the other, the two things are equal to each other. Although these arguments were initially proposed in the context of discussions against the possibility of infinities, they have played pivotal roles in the historical evolution of the notion of INFINITIES OF DIFFERENT SIZES.

Keywords: infinity, medieval philosophy, finitism, the mapping argument, the equality argument

ISBNs: 9781009618434 (HB), 9781009048507 (PB), 9781009047623 (OC)
ISSNs: 2399-2883 (online), 2514-3808 (print)

Contents

1 Introduction

Philosophers have always been tantalised by the notion of INFINITY and the complicated puzzles that it raises in various philosophical contexts. The nature and characteristics of the infinite and how (if at all) it can be instantiated in the world have been the subject of long-standing philosophical discussions. Philosophers of different eras and traditions of thought have engaged with the infinite through various approaches and from different perspectives. But there is no doubt that some of the most exciting episodes of such engagements have occurred in the medieval traditions of Jewish, Christian, and Islamic philosophy. Philosophers from these traditions discussed a wide variety of issues regarding the notion of INFINITY and its instances in the world (if any). Medieval encounters with the notion of INFINITY have various aspects and can be approached from different angles. Medieval arguments for the impossibility of one or another sort of infinity form one such aspect. Some of the most significant ideas about infinity, which have played a crucial role in the evolution of our understanding of this notion, were introduced and/or developed in the context of the medieval arguments for finitism. In the wide spectrum of these arguments, those that are related, in one way or another, to the problem of the possibility of infinities of different sizes seem to have significant historical and philosophical connections to our modern concept of infinity. Nevertheless, many aspects of the historical development of such arguments and their philosophical significance are still unexplored. This Element aims to shed light on previously uninvestigated corners of medieval finitism by discussing two main groups of the most important medieval arguments that engage with the notion of INFINITIES OF DIFFERENT SIZES.[1] Given this specific scope, I refrain from engaging with medieval arguments for infinitism in general or for the existence of infinities of different sizes in particular.[2]

My focus in this study is primarily on the *mathematical* aspects of medieval finitism. However, it is important to note that extensive discussions of finitism can rarely (if at all) be found in medieval *mathematical* works. Medieval scholars usually investigated the infinite in either the works of *theology* and *metaphysics* (in connection to issues like the eternity of creation, arguments for the existence of God, the infinity of a chain of causally related elements, and the infinity of the objects of God's knowledge or power) or the works of *physics* (in connection to issues like the infinity of the world, the infinity and continuity of motion, the infinity of power, the atomistic structure of the material world,

[1] For two seminal studies focused on historical engagements with the idea of infinities of different sizes, see Davenport (1999) and Mancosu (2009).

[2] Such arguments are extensively discussed in Mancosu (forthcoming).

and the existence of vacuum). That is why the primary concern of many medieval arguments discussed in this Element is not mathematical. Nevertheless, we cannot reach a comprehensive picture of the historical evolution of the notion of MATHEMATICAL INFINITY without careful analyses of these arguments.

This Element is structured as follows. Section 2 illustrates the definition and some of the characteristics that medieval philosophers typically considered for infinity under the influence of the ancient Greek philosophers and, in particular, Aristotle (d. 322 BCE). In the same section, I also discuss some (though by no means all) significant distinctions regarding the various types of infinities that medieval philosophers employed to develop their theories of infinities. Without a precise understanding of those distinctions, we cannot easily detect subtle differences among diverse medieval approaches to finitism. Different versions of what I call 'the Equality Argument' are discussed in Section 3. This argument relies on the assumption that there cannot be infinities of different sizes. Although this assumption does not sound true from our contemporary perspective, it was accepted by many ancient and medieval philosophers. Section 4 provides a detailed analysis of another influential finitist argument, which is usually called 'the Mapping Argument'. The mature version of the Mapping Argument was presented by Ibn Sīnā (d. 1037) – who was referred to in the Latin tradition by 'Avicenna' – through the refinement of an earlier, less accurate version by al-Kindī (d. 870). The philosophical significance of the main ideas developed in the context of debates concerning the soundness of these arguments and their relevance to our contemporary conception of mathematical infinity will be discussed in Section 5, where this Element concludes.

Before closing this introduction, I must clarify that although this Element addresses all three medieval Jewish, Christian, and Islamic traditions of philosophy, my primary focus is on the Islamic tradition. This is not only because I am more familiar with this tradition but also because of two other things. First, in the secondary literature in Western languages, medieval Arabic-Islamic theories of infinity are studied no more than their Jewish counterparts and far less than the Christian ones. Second, and more importantly, the most significant discussions of the Equality and Mapping Arguments in Jewish and Christian philosophy are historically posterior to and, in many cases, inspired by earlier discussions of these arguments in the Islamic tradition. In each subsequent section, I analyse the views of medieval thinkers in historical order. As we will see, Muslim figures take precedence in many of these sections. Admittedly, many sophisticated discussions of infinity in the other two traditions have had no anticipation in the Islamic tradition. For example, many of the arguments discussed in the fourteenth-century Latin philosophy (usually considered the most important period of the medieval debates about infinity) have no counterparts in the Islamic tradition. However, I do not discuss those arguments in this Element because, as I have already mentioned, I am mainly concerned with the Equality and Mapping Arguments.

2 Definition and Characteristics of Infinity

Infinitude is limitlessness. However, limitlessness can be understood in two different ways. As Fakhr al-Dīn al-Rāzī (d. 1210), a Muslim theologian and philosopher, puts it:

> T1. Al-Rāzī (1990, *Eastern Investigations*, vol. 1, p. 297)
>
> What is literally said [to be limitless] is said either in the way of simple negation (*al-salb*) or in the way of metathetic affirmation (*al-ʿudūl*). As for what is said in the way of simple negation, it [i.e., to say that it is limitless in the way of simple negation] is to take away from that thing the meaning because of which it is correct to describe that thing as having a limit. And that [meaning] is quantity. This is like what is said of God Most High that He is limitless and of the point that it is limitless. As for what is [said to be limitless] in the way of metathetic affirmation, there is something because of which it is [in principle] correct to describe that thing as having a realised limit, but no limit is [in fact] realised.[3]

According to this passage, limitlessness can be understood in two different senses. A thing can be limitless because it lacks quantity. Such a thing is not capable of having a limit. Thus, it would be a category mistake to talk about the limit of it. In the same sense that talking about the colour of justice is a category mistake, talking about the limit of God or of a point is a category mistake. The limitlessness of such things must be taken in the way of simple negation. Limit is by no means attributable to such things. By contrast, things that possess quantity can, in principle, have a limit. Now, if such a thing – for example, a line – has no limit, the limitlessness of it must be understood through metathetic affirmation. To better grasp the distinction made in the passage, consider the sentences ‘justice is colourless’ and ‘the glass is colourless’. The former sentence – assuming that it is true – expresses a simple negation because justice cannot have a colour. Colour is by no means attributable to justice. However, the latter sentence can be interpreted as expressing a metathetic affirmation because the glass has no colour while, in principle, it could have a colour.[4] In our discussion of infinity, we are concerned with things that are

---

[3] Unless otherwise mentioned, all the translations from Arabic and Persian are mine. Accordingly, when I cite a work that includes both an original text in Arabic or Persian and its English translation, the page numbers refer to the Arabic or Persian part of the cited work.

[4] The origin of the distinction between simple negation and metathetic affirmation is Aristotle’s *De Interpretatione* 10. To see how this distinction is usually understood in the context of the

limitless in the sense of metathetic affirmation. These are the things that are unlimited, though they could have been limited.

T1 alludes to the general point that, in the framework of the Aristotelian categories, infinity must be considered an attribute of quantities. Quantities are either discrete or continuous. Number and language are examples of discrete quantities; and line, surface, body, time, and place are examples of continuous quantities (*Categories* 6, 4b20–25).[5] Thus, roughly speaking, infinity must be considered an attribute of *magnitudes* and *multitudes*.[6] According to Aristotle, 'something is infinite if, taking it quantity by quantity, we can always take something outside' (*Physics* III.6, 207a7–8). This definition seems to be universally accepted by medieval philosophers. Some of them explicitly endorsed this definition – or some paraphrase of it – in their works. To give a couple of examples, Ibn Sīnā (2009, *The Physics of* The Healing, chapter III.7, § 3) contends that infinite things are those which 'whatever you take from them, you always find something outside of them'.[7] Instead of appealing to a repetitive process of taking from infinity, Ibn Sīnā defines infinity by

---

Aristotelian logic, consider a sentence '*a* is not F'. If this sentence is understood as expressing a simple negation, then it says that it is not the case that *a* is F. Thus, the sentence in question can be true regardless of whether *a* exists and whether it is capable of having F or not-F as a property. On the other hand, if that sentence is taken as expressing a metathetic affirmation, then it says that it is the case that *a* is not-F. Given the existential import of the affirmative claims, this sentence is true only if all the following conditions are satisfied: (a) *a* exists, (b) F and not-F are in principle attributable to *a* (or, equivalently, *a* is in principle capable of being F or not-F), and (c) as a matter of fact, a does have the property of not-F. Regarding the engagements of the philosophers of the classical period of Islamic philosophy with this distinction, see Thom (2008), Hodges (2012), and Kaukua (2020). The first paper addresses the account of al-Fārābī (d. 950), and the latter two focus on the view of Ibn Sīnā, which was the primary source for the majority of discussions concerning this distinction in the postclassical Islamic philosophy.

5 All the translations of Aristotle's terms and phrases are borrowed from Aristotle (1984, *The Complete Works of Aristotle*). In this specific translation, 'language' is taken to be the translation of the Greek term 'λόγος'. Other translators have selected 'speech' as the translation of this term. In any case, as it is explicitly mentioned in *Categories* 6, 4b32, what Aristotle here means by 'λόγος' is the spoken language, which is constituted of a series of sounds and can be 'measured by long and short syllables'. So, it is comprised of distinct units that can be counted. This might explain why language is considered a discrete quantity. Nevertheless, many scholars believe that it is not really clear why language must be included in discrete quantities. This unclarity is intensified by the fact that there is no reference to language in Aristotle's discussion of categories in *Metaphysics* V.13. 1020a7–32. On Aristotle's account of quantity, see, among others, Studtmann (2004).

6 Hereafter, for the sake of simplicity and unless otherwise specified, by a 'magnitude', I mean a straight line that represents a one-dimensional magnitude (e.g., weight or distance). Accordingly, by 'the length of a magnitude', I mean the length of the line that represents that magnitude. By setting a convention and taking a magnitude of a certain finite length as our measuring unit, we can represent numbers by magnitudes: number *n* can be represented by a magnitude of the length of *n* units. However, the possibility of making such conventions does not undermine the fact that magnitudes in themselves are continuous quantities. I will later clarify how a 'multitude' must be understood.

7 See also Ibn Sīnā (2009, *The Physics of* The Healing, chapter III.7, § 2 and chapter III.9, § 1). For Ibn Sīnā's definition of infinity, see McGinnis (2010, section 4) and Zarepour (2020, section 2).

a single take. He says that infinity is such that no matter how big what you take from it is, something remains. Although it is not explicitly stated, it must be assumed that what is taken is itself finite. The same definition, with a slightly different phrasing, is endorsed by Fakhr al-Dīn al-Rāzī (1990, *Eastern Investigations*, vol. 1, p. 297–98): an infinity is such that 'when you take whatever amount of it that you wish, you find something outside of it without the need for returning [what is taken]'. By adding the phrase 'without the need for returning', he probably means that you can take more and more from an infinity, and even if what is taken is never returned, there always remains something other than what has been taken so far.

Other medieval philosophers either did not provide any explicit definition of infinity or offered other definitions that are somehow compatible with the Aristotelian definition of infinity. We will soon visit some of such definitions. Nevertheless, to the best of my knowledge, there was no significant criticism of the Aristotelian definition of infinity in medieval philosophy. At least not when we are only concerned with physical and mathematical infinity without touching on other things, for example, the qualitative infinity of God. The Aristotelian definition seems to be compatible with all the medieval discussions of infinity that are investigated in the following sections.

Aristotle makes two crucial distinctions about infinity. One between infinity *by addition* and *by division*, and the other between *actual* and *potential* infinity (*Physics* III.6, 206a14–25). Roughly speaking, a totality is infinite by addition if and only if it is (or at least can be conceived as being) formed by the successive addition of parts each of which has a similar finite quantity (or, less technically, size). For example, a straight line AB that starts from A and extends infinitely in the direction of B is infinite by addition because it can be conceived as being formed by the successive addition of a segment of a finite length, such as d (Fig. 1a).[8] On the other hand, a totality is infinite by division if, with no limit, it can be successively divided into smaller parts. For example, a finite line CD can be halved infinitely many times by being successively divided at D_1, D_2, D_3, . . . so that, for every $n \geq 1$, $CD_n = 2CD_{n+1}$ (Fig. 1b). CD is infinite by division but not by addition. To explain the idea of infinity by division using the aforementioned Aristotelian definition of infinity, it can be said that

[8] To be accurate, this form of referring to an infinite line is misleading and incompatible with the standards of modern mathematics. This is because it leaves the impression that 'B' – in the same manner as 'A' – refers to a point. However, this should not be the case because otherwise 'AB' refers to a finite line segment that is bounded with A and B. Nevertheless, this is how infinite lines are referred to in many medieval texts. See, for example, T14. Thus, I remain faithful to their reference style, hoping that the contexts of the following discussions of infinite lines will spare the readers from potential misunderstanding caused by this style. In visualisation, the bounded side of a line is represented by a bullet point and the infinitely extending side of it by an arrow point.

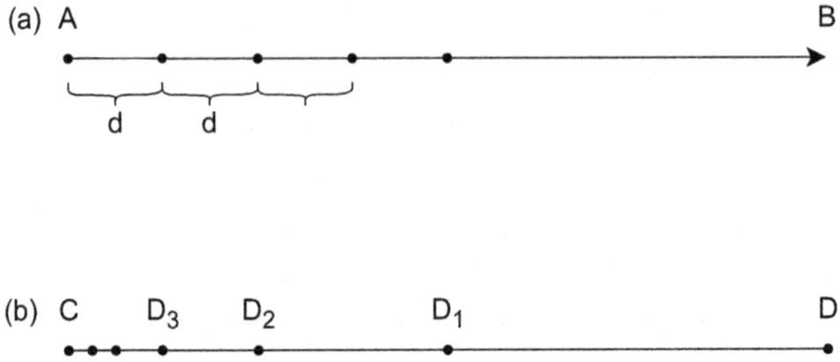

Figure 1 Infinity by addition and infinity by division.

a magnitude is infinite by division if and only if, no matter how many times you divide it into smaller parts, it is always possible to make a further division. The distinction between infinity by addition and by division provides a conceptual tool to differentiate the talk of infinitely big things from that of infinitely small things. This explains the natural association of the notion of INFINITY BY DIVISION with that of CONTINUITY. But what we are concerned with in this Element is mainly infinity by addition. More precisely, the primary aim of the two types of finitist arguments discussed in this study is to reject the possibility of certain sorts of infinity by addition.[9]

In broad terms, if the process of addition or division by which an infinity is formed is already completed and all the parts or components of that infinity coexist simultaneously, then that infinity is *actual*; otherwise, it is *potential*. If a magnitude is being extended infinitely by successively adding segments of a certain length while its current length is finite, then that line is only potentially infinite. Similarly, if a finite magnitude is, in principle, divisible into infinitely many parts but is not yet so divided, its infinity (i.e., the infinitude of the multitude of all its division) must be considered potential, or so Aristotle suggested.[10] As we will see in the following sections, the distinction between actual and potential infinity plays a crucial role in the medieval accounts of infinity. However, it is important to note that not all medieval philosophers share similar interpretations of the notions of ACTUALITY and POTENTIALITY. As a result of various modifications that medieval philosophers proposed to these notions, there are examples of

[9] However, it must be noted that if something is infinite by division, the number of the divisions that can be made in that thing is infinite by addition. So, the notions of INFINITY BY DIVISION and INFINITY BY ADDITION, though distinct, are related to each other. The relation between these two conceptions of infinity is clearly visible in passages like T2 and T3.

[10] Aristotle's conception of infinity is studied, among others, by Hintikka (1966), Lear (1980), Kouremenos (1995), Bowin (2007), Coope (2012), Nawar (2015), and Cooper (2016).

infinite totalities that are taken as actual infinities by some philosophers and as potential infinities by others.[11]

Along with these distinctions about various types of infinity, we should take note of some of the most important characteristics that medieval philosophers considered for infinity. In particular, there are two ideas about infinity that many medieval views regarding the size of infinity are developed either based on or in reaction to them. The first idea goes as follows:

Equality of Infinities (EI): All comparable infinities are equal to each other. No infinity is greater or lesser than another.

In the next section, we will see that the long history of the discussions of infinity in which this idea or something in its vicinity is presupposed goes back at least to Lucretius (d. circa 55 BCE). **EI** was accepted as an incontrovertible axiom by many medieval philosophers. One might think that, for example, the infinite benevolence of God is not comparable to an infinite line considered in geometry. They are not of the same species. Nor can they be compared to each other quantitatively. Thus, it does not make sense to ask which one is greater, or so one might contend. However, different infinite geometrical lines are of the same species and comparable to each other. Therefore, if **EI** is true, we must conclude that no infinite line can be greater or lesser than the others. They are all equal to each other. To put it more cautiously, they are all of the same size. In general, in the context of the forthcoming discussions, when it is said that two things are equal, it merely means that those things are equal in terms of quantity.

A rationale behind **EI** could be that if something is infinite, it must be limitless. Moreover, if something is limitless, it must, in a sense, encompass everything. So, nothing can be greater than an infinity. Not even another infinity can surpass it. As it is stated by John Philoponus (d. 570) in his *Against Aristotle on the Eternity of the World* (2014, fr. 132, p. 144), it is 'impossible that ⟨anything⟩ should be greater than the infinite, or that the infinite should be increased'.[12] Also, **EI** might

[11] An important medieval distinction that I do not touch on in this Element is the distinction between the *categorematic* and *syncategorematic* senses of infinity, which is closely related to the distinction between *actual* and *potential* infinities. On the origin of the distinction between categorematic and syncategorematic infinities and its role in the medieval Latin discussions of the theories of infinity and continuity, see, among others, Geach (1967), Kretzmann (1982), Murdoch (1982, pp. 567–68), Duhem (1985, chapter 1), Uckelman (2015), and Moore (2019, section 3.3).

[12] The angle brackets are by the translator. The original text of *Against Aristotle* is lost. Nevertheless, a large part of this treatise is now reconstructed based on the fragments quoted in Greek, Arabic, and, in one case, Syriac sources. The most reliable fragments are those quoted by Simplicius (d. 560), who had access to the original treatise, in his commentaries on Aristotle's *Physics* and *On the Heavens*. Fortunately, Simplicius's quotes form the largest portion of the reconstructed treatise.

be motivated by some conceptions of the infinity of God. In theological contexts, it is usually assumed that the only real and absolute infinity is God. God is the unsurpassable being with respect to whom everything else is limited and finite. If so, absolute infinity is a unique thing that cannot be greater or lesser. That is perhaps why some theologians – for example, the Franciscan Roger Bacon (d. 1292) in his *Opus Majus* (1928, vol. II, p. 798) – have defined infinity as 'that to which nothing can be added'.

The second crucial idea about infinity, which can be detected in the background of remarkable ancient and medieval discussions of infinity, states that infinity must be treated as a number:

Numericality of Infinite Multitudes (NIM): For every multitude X, the following claims are equivalent to each other: (a) X is an infinite multitude; (b) the number of the members of X is infinite; and (c) there is an infinite number describing how many members X has.

It is noteworthy that, in medieval discussions of infinity, when a *multitude* of things (e.g., numbers, points, human beings, and revolutions of celestial bodies) is referred to, it is typically considered collectively as a *whole* whose smallest *parts* are its *members*.[13] Accordingly, although every member of a multitude is a part of it, the other way around does not necessarily hold. For example, the multitude of odd numbers is a *submultitude* and, consequently, a part of the multitude of natural numbers, though not a member of it. This is roughly how the notions of MULTITUDE, SUBMULTITUDE, and MEMBERSHIP mentioned in **NIM** and in the following analyses must be read.

It must also be emphasised that **NIM** has no specific implication for the ontological status of the infinite numbers it is referring to. The mere claim that there is an infinite number, describing how many members a certain infinite multitude has, does not say anything about the nature of that infinite number. In particular, it does not commit us to a realist/Platonist account of the ontology of infinite numbers. The claim in question can be read coherently in a nominalist way. As a result, people with different views regarding the ontology of mathematical objects can share the same view regarding the plausibility of **NIM**.

If we accept **NIM**, then **EI** can be understood as implying that there is a unique infinite number, say *I*, such that the number of the members of every

[13] Apparently, some medieval philosophers were aware that a group of objects can be considered in two different ways, one distributively and another collectively (something like the mereological sum of certain elements). For example, such a distinction can be detected in Ibn Sīnā's famous Proof of the Sincere for the existence of God. See Świętorzecka *et al.* (forthcoming). The difference between *distributive* and *collective* considerations of a multitude corresponds to the Russellian distinction between *class as one* and *class as many* (if we interpret multitudes as classes). See Russell (2010 [1903], section 70).

infinite multitude is *I*. No infinite multitude can have more or less than *I* members. However, it is worth noting that **NIM** on its own does not imply the existence of either any infinite multitude or any infinite number. For example, as we will shortly see, some medieval philosophers endorse **NIM** and argue that there can be no infinite multitude of objects because there can be no infinite number.

One might think that presupposing **NIM** is necessary when applying **EI** to infinite multitudes. However, this is not the case. If we believe that multitudes are comparable (in terms of greatness or, simply, size) solely through the comparison of the numbers describing how many members they have, then **EI** is not applicable to multitudes unless we accept **NIM**. However, it is coherent to contend that multitudes are comparable to each other even if some of them lack numbers describing how many members they have. This suggests that, in principle, one can deny **NIM** without denying the applicability of **EI** to infinite multitudes/magnitudes. That is why I formulated these principles independently. Having said that, we know from modern logic and set theory that if we accept that there is a way to compare the sizes of infinities to say whether or not they are equal to each other, then it is possible to introduce infinite numbers. One way to do this is by employing an *abstraction principle*. Thus, if we find that principle plausible (or, more precisely, if we accept that applying such an abstraction principle to infinities is legitimate), the existence of comparable infinities implies the existence of infinite numbers. It must be noted, however, that infinite numbers can be defined even without using such principles.[14] Nevertheless, we do not need these technical considerations to discuss medieval accounts of infinity that were much more naïve than ours.

EI and **NIM** have been addressed in many ancient and medieval exchanges on infinity. As counterintuitive as they might seem from the viewpoint of contemporary mathematics, they were endorsed by many ancient and medieval philosophers. In particular, these principles were employed in some of the most influential medieval arguments against the existence of actual infinity. In the next section, we discuss an argument for finitism in which **EI** plays a crucial role. An extensive investigation of the engagements of several medieval philosophers with this argument can help us have a better understanding of medieval approaches to the problem of infinities of different sizes.

Before commencing our discussion of the first argument for finitism, it must be noted, as a general caveat, that there are so many subtle differences between various medieval views regarding the possibility of actual infinity that cannot be accurately represented by the coarse-grained distinction between finitism and

[14] On defining infinite numbers with or without employing abstraction principles, see Mancosu (2016).

infinitism. For example, not everyone who is finitist about the material realm also denies the possibility of the presence of infinities in the mind and/or in the realm of the mind-independent immaterial entities (e.g., souls). Moreover, finitists do not necessarily have similar conceptions of actual infinity. As a result, an infinity that is actual for a philosopher might not be considered actual by another. That is why one philosopher might reject the existence of an infinity accepted by another while both insist that actual infinity does not exist. These differences are perfectly reflected in the finitist arguments proposed by medieval philosophers. Regrettably, space limits prevent us from covering many such arguments. Our focus would be on different versions of two finitist arguments which play a pivotal role in the history of philosophical investigations about infinities of different sizes.

3 The Equality Argument

As I mentioned earlier, the history of the arguments against the existence of actual infinities by appealing to **EI** goes back to at least Lucretius. Arguing in favour of atomism, he writes:

> T2. Lucretius (2001, *On the Nature of Things*, Book I, 615–30, p. 58)
>
> [I]f there is no smallest point, every minutest body will be composed of an infinite number of parts (*parvissima quaeque corpora constabunt ex partibus infinitis*), since a half of a half will always have a half and there will be no limit to the possibility of division. If this is the case, what will distinguish the whole universe from the smallest thing in it? Nothing; for, no matter how fully infinite is the whole universe, the minutest objects will equally be composed of an infinite number of parts (*parvissima quae sunt, ex infinitis constabunt partibus aeque*). But since sound judgment loudly protests against this conclusion and denies that the mind can believe it, you must admit defeat and acknowledge the existence of points that have no parts and are the smallest things; and this being so, you must also acknowledge the existence of solid and everlasting primary elements.

The most plausible reconstruction of the argument presented in T2 seems to be something like the following:

(1) If there is no indivisible part, then every object is composed of an infinite number of parts.
(2) If every object has an infinite number of parts, then the minutest objects and the whole universe are composed of an equal number of parts.
(3) The minutest objects and the whole universe are not composed of an equal number of parts.

Therefore:

(4) It is not the case that there is no indivisible part.

EI seems to be a hidden assumption of this argument. In particular, (2) does not hold unless **EI** is true. The mere fact that the whole universe and the minutest objects are composed of an infinite number of parts does not imply that they have the same number of parts unless we assume that all infinite multitudes are of the same size.

Plutarch (d. circa 120) has offered a similar argument in favour of atomism in which **EI** is more explicitly presented. In a harsh criticism of Stoic anti-atomism, Plutarch writes:

> T3. Plutarch (1976, *Against the Stoics on Common Conceptions*, 1079a, p. 813)
>
> For it would not be possible to conceive one magnitude as greater or less than another if for the parts of both alike it is characteristic to proceed to infinity; but the nature of inequality is abolished, for, when things are conceived as unequal, it is by the ultimate parts that the one leaves off before the other and the other passes it by and is in excess of it. And, if inequality does not exist, it follows that unevenness does not exist or roughness of body either, for unevenness is inequality of a single surface with itself and roughness is unevenness along with hardness, none of which is left by those who bring no body to an end in an ultimate part but in number of parts extend all bodies to infinity. Yet is it not completely clear that a man consists of more parts than the man's finger does and the universe again of more parts than does the man? This all men know and have in mind if they have not become Stoics; but, once they have become Stoics, their statements and opinions are to the contrary effect that the man is not made up of more parts than the finger is or the universe of more parts than the man, for by division bodies are triturated to infinity and among infinites none is more or less and none exceeds another in multitude at all or else the parts of the one exceeded would stop being divided and making multitudes of themselves.

Arguments of the same spirit were later developed in the context of the debates concerning the temporal origination of the world. Criticising Aristotle and Proclus (d. 485), John Philoponus has offered a series of arguments against the eternity of the world. According to some of these arguments that are based on **EI**, the world is not eternal in the sense of having no temporal beginning because otherwise there would have been infinities of different sizes.[15] Since **EI** rules out the possibility of such infinities, we have to reject the eternity of the

[15] Throughout this Element, 'eternity' and 'eternal' must be taken as meaning, respectively, *temporal beginninglessness* and *temporally beginningless*.

world, or so Philoponus contends. An argument developed based on this general pattern goes as follows:

> T4. Philoponus (2004, *Against Proclus On the Eternity of the World*, chapter 1, section 3, p. 24–25)
>
> And if the world had no beginning and the number of men living before, say, Socrates was infinite, and those living from Socrates until the present time have been added to it, there will be something greater than the infinite, which is impossible. And if the number of men that have lived is infinite, the number of horses that have lived is certainly also infinite. [So] you will be doubling the infinite again. [And] if you add to these the number of dogs as well, you will triple the infinite, and if each of the other [species] is added it will be multiplied many times over. And this is among the greatest of impossibilities, for it is not possible to be greater than the infinite, not to mention many times greater.

Like many other ancient and medieval thinkers, Philoponus believes that the beginninglessness of the world implies the beginninglessness of the generation of every species, including human beings. This means that if the world is beginningless, the collection of all the members of any species that have lived until a specific time is infinite. T4 aims to show that this consequence is controversial. If the world had no beginning, the number of men living before Socrates would have been infinite. However, the number of men who have lived until the present time is greater than the number of men living before Socrates. As a result, the beginninglessness of the world implies the existence of infinities of different sizes. This contradicts **EI**. So, the world must have a beginning. Moreover, if the world has no temporal beginning, not only the number of men who have lived until the present time but also the number of horses or dogs or members of any other species is infinite. This implies that the number of men and horses who have lived so far is double the number of men who have lived so far. Similarly, the number of men, horses, and dogs who have lived so far is triple the number of men who have lived so far. This again contradicts EI because it implies that there are infinities of different sizes. Accordingly, the assumption of the eternity of the world must be rejected.

There is no doubt that Philoponus's arguments in T4 appeal to **EI**. But it seems to me that he also presupposes **NIM**. In this passage, Philoponus refers to numbers associated with infinite collections by stating that if the world has no beginning, then, for example, 'the number (*ὁ ἀριθμός*/*ho arithmos*) of men . . . is infinite'. This leaves the impression that he accepts that the existence of infinite multitudes implies the existence of infinite numbers. Equivalently, it might mean that Philoponus accepts **NIM** (or something close to it). However, one could object to this line of reasoning by reading '*arithmos*' differently. More specifically, one might take '*arithmos*' simply as 'collection', 'plurality' or, to use our own terminology, 'multitude'. In this reading, the claim that *the number of men is infinite* implies nothing other than that *the multitude of men is infinite.* However, the latter claim does not imply the existence of an infinite number. Accordingly, the mere fact that Philoponus says that the number of men is infinite does not justify the claim that he endorses **NIM**. Thus, we need other pieces of evidence to establish Philoponus's commitment to **NIM**.[16]

It seems to me that a convincing sign of such a commitment is that Philoponus talks about *the infinite* and the possibility of multiplying it. It is legitimate to ask what the reference of 'the infinite' is in T4. It is obvious that 'the infinite' does not refer to a certain infinite collection of things (e.g., men, horses, or dogs). Philoponus states that by considering the multitude of the horses that have lived so far, in addition to the multitude of the men who have lived so far, we are doubling *the infinite.* He then adds that by considering similar multitudes of other species we can multiply *the infinite* many times over. Even if we can make sense of multiplying a multitude, what Philoponus talks about in T4 is not multiplying an infinite multitude itself. Rather, he talks about multiplying the *size* of an infinite multitude. What he refers to by 'the infinite' is the *size* of an infinite collection. On the one hand, accepting **EI**, he believes that all infinite multitudes must be of the same size. So, the size of any infinite multitude must be *the infinite.* On the other hand, by considering the multitudes he mentioned, we can think of infinite multitudes whose sizes are multiplications of *the infinite.* To get rid of this contradiction, we should give up the assumption of the eternity of the world, or so Philoponus thinks.

It must be noted that Philoponus does not talk merely about different infinite multitudes some of which are greater than others. He specifically talks about multiplying *the infinite.* He takes *the infinite* as something that (a) describes the size of an infinite multitude and (b) can be multiplied according to the examples he discussed. Thus, it seems that he treats *the infinite* as if it is a number. That is why I think Philoponus endorses **NIM**. Indeed, if **NIM** and **EI** are true, then there is a unique infinite number, say I, such that the number of the members of any infinite multitude is I. The reference of 'the infinite' in T4 seems to be such an I. T4 can be interpreted as arguing that the eternity of the past is incompatible with the conjunction of **NIM** and **EI**. The conjunction of **NIM** and **EI** implies that the size of every infinite multitude must be I. However, the eternity of the world implies that there can be infinite multitudes whose sizes are not just greater than I but even multiplications of I. More precisely, if the world has no

[16] In *Physics* IV.11, 219b4–6, Aristotle distinguishes two senses of *arithmos*: what is counted (i.e., multitude or collection) and what by which we count (i.e., number). I am thankful to a reviewer who drew my attention to Aristotle's passage and raised the abovementioned objection.

beginning, the number of men living before Socrates is *I*. However, the number of men who have lived until the present time is greater than the number of men living before Socrates. As a result, there is something greater than *I*. Moreover, if the world is beginningless, not only the number of men who have lived until the present time but also the number of horses or dogs or members of any other species is *I*. This implies that the number of men and horses who have lived so far is 2*I*, and the number of men, horses, and dogs who have lived so far is 3*I*. Considering other species, we can see that *I* can be multiplied many more times. These results are incompatible with **EI**. Thus, we have to reject the eternity of the world.[17] If this reading of T4 is correct, then when Philoponus talks about the number of men, horses, dogs, and so on, he does not talk about the collection of those things. Rather, he talks about the number that describes the size of the collection in question.

Considering the arguments of Philoponus in T4, one might wonder how we can establish the premise that the number of men who have lived until the present time is greater than the number of men living before Socrates. Philoponus seems to take this premise for granted. He does not provide any explicit justification for it. Nevertheless, in later discussions of structurally similar arguments, the relevant counterparts of the aforementioned premise are justified by appealing to the fifth *common notion* from the first book of Euclid's *The Elements* (1908, vol. 1, p. 155). This common notion, which rejects the possibility of whole-part equality, goes as follows:

Common Notion 5 (CN5): The whole is greater than the part.

Here (and unless otherwise specified in what follows), 'part' should be understood as a *proper* part. This is because there are mereologies in which *parthood* is a reflexive relation, in the sense that everything is a part of itself (Sider 2007, pp. 60 and 70), wherein every whole W includes a part equal to W, which falsifies **CN5**. Thus, to preserve the truth of **CN5**, we should take it as referring to the relation of *proper parthood*, which is, by definition, irreflexive. Nothing

[17] The arguments presented in T4 are based on the claim that the infinitude of the past implies the beginninglessness of the generation of any species and the infinitude of the multitude of the particulars of any species that have come into existence until any specific time. However, those arguments can also be reconstructed based on the weaker claim that the *possibility* of the infinitude of the past implies (a) the *possibility* of the beginninglessness of the generation of such species and, consequently, (b) the *possibility* of the infinitude of those multitudes. To do this, it suffices to appeal to a modal reading of **EI**, stating that it is *impossible* for infinities to be of different sizes. On this interpretation, **EI** rejects not only the existence of infinities of different sizes but also the *possibility* of the existence of such infinities. Accordingly, **EI** is incompatible with even the *possibility* of the infinitude of the past, regardless of whether or not, as a matter of *fact*, the infinitude of the past implies the existence of infinities of different sizes.

can be a proper part of itself. Understood as such, **CN5** states that every whole is greater than any of its proper parts.

An immediate consequence of **CN5** is that every magnitude is greater than any of its submagnitudes (i.e., the magnitudes obtained by removing a part of the initial magnitude). Moreover, since multitudes are interpreted as having a whole-part relationship with their submultitudes, **CN5** implies that every multitude is greater than any of its proper submultitudes. Now, note that the multitude of men living before Socrates is a proper submultitude and, consequently, a part of the multitude of men living until the present time. Thus, according to **CN5**, the latter multitude must be greater than the former. This means that the number of men who have lived until the present time is greater than the number of men living before Socrates. Thus, the premise in question is established.[18]

In a vague categorisation, I take any particular finitist argument which relies on the conjunction of **CN5** and **EI** as a version of what I call 'the Equality Argument'. The general aim of the Equality Argument for finitism is to establish the impossibility of the infinite wholes some of whose parts are also infinite.[19] Given **CN5**, the existence of such infinite wholes and parts implies that there are infinities some of which are greater than others. However, this contradicts **EI**. Accordingly, the infinite wholes in question must be regarded as impossible.

In another group of arguments, Philoponus argues against the eternity of the world by appealing to the Aristotelian idea of the untraversability of infinity. According to Aristotle (*Physics* VI.7, 238a20–31), no infinity can be traversed. This principle implies that (a) an infinite magnitude cannot be passed over, and (b) the members of an infinite multitude cannot be counted entirely. The core idea behind Philoponus's finitist arguments from untraversability is that the world cannot be beginningless because otherwise some infinities would have been traversed until the present time. In one such argument, he argues that if the world has no beginning, there is an infinite collection of humans who have so far come into existence one after another, as if an infinity of humans has been counted out unit by unit. Philoponus takes this as that an infinity has been

[18] It seems that the claims (a) the minutest objects and the whole universe are not composed of an equal number of parts (i.e., a premise of Lucretius's argument in T2), and (b) the universe has more parts than the man, and the man more than the man's finger (i.e., a premise of Plutarch's argument in T3) must similarly be justified by appealing to **CN5**.

[19] Does it make sense to talk about infinite wholes that do not have infinite parts? If it does not, the Equality Argument aims to establish the impossibility of infinite wholes by appealing to CN5 and EI. However, following a conservative approach, I prefer not to take a position regarding the answer to the aforementioned question. Therefore, I take the target of the attack of the Equality Argument to be those infinite wholes some of whose parts are also infinite. Such a domain of wholes might or might not include all infinite wholes, depending on the correct answer to that question.

traversed. Since this contradicts the untraversability of infinity, the idea of the eternity of the world is untenable and must be rejected. Put differently, if the world has no temporal beginning, any individual X is the last ring of at least one infinite chain of human beings, each of whom is a child of the previous one. So, the existence of X in a world whose past is infinite means that an infinity has been traversed. However, if infinity is untraversable, the existence of X implies the finitude of any chain of its ancestors and, consequently, the finitude of the past. Developing such a line of argument, Philoponus (2004, *Against Proclus*, chapter 1, section 3, p. 24) contends that 'the number of earlier individuals is not infinite. For [if it were] the generations of the race would not have reached down to each of us, for it is impossible to traverse the infinite'.[20] In another line of argument, he contends that if the world is eternal, then the infinite has been traversed until the present time, not only once but many times. But if the infinite cannot be traversed once, then a fortiori cannot be traversed many times. This argument is presented as follows:

> T5. Philoponus (2014, *Against Aristotle*, fr. 132, p. 146)
>
> [I]f the motion of the heavens is without a beginning, ⟨then⟩ it is necessary that the sphere of Saturn has rotated with an infinite ⟨number of⟩ revolutions, but the ⟨sphere⟩ of Jupiter with nearly three times more ⟨revolutions⟩ than that. The ⟨revolutions⟩ of the sun will be thirty times greater ⟨in number⟩ than the ones of Saturn, the ⟨revolutions⟩ of the moon 360 times, and the ⟨revolutions⟩ of the sphere of the fixed stars more than ten thousand times greater. But how, if it is not ⟨even⟩ possible to traverse the infinite once, is it not beyond all absurdity to assume ten thousand times the infinite, or rather the infinite an infinite number of times? In consequence, it is necessary [. . .] that the circular motion of the heavens did not exist before ⟨but⟩ had a beginning of existence.[21]

The argument explicitly mentioned in T5 is based on the idea of the untraversability of infinity. However, T5 can also inspire another argument against the eternity of the world, which is based on **NIM** and **EI**.[22] This argument that I call 'the argument from the numbers of the revolutions of celestial bodies' goes like this: recall the assumption that the number of the members of any infinite multitude is *I*. If the world has no beginning, then the number of revolutions of Saturn is *I*. However, during each of Saturn's revolutions, Jupiter, the sun,

[20] The square brackets are by the translator.

[21] The square brackets of this quote are mine. The angle brackets are by the translator.

[22] In fact, I mentioned T5 just to discuss the argument that is based on **EI**, rather than the one that is based on the untraversability of infinity. Medieval philosophers have developed a large number of finitist arguments from untraversability. Nevertheless, since those arguments are rarely concerned with the problem of infinities of different sizes, I have not touched on them in this Element.

and the moon respectively complete 3, 30, and 360 revolutions. This indicates that if the world is beginningless, the number of revolutions of Saturn, Jupiter, the sun, and the moon must respectively be I, $3I$, $30I$, and $360I$. Since this outcome is incompatible with **EI**, the eternity of the world must be given up.

Medieval philosophers employed these ideas by Lucretius, Plutarch, and Philoponus in arguments for various purposes.[23] Nevertheless, many of those philosophers did not know the exact origins of the employed ideas. In the early Arabic philosophy, a version of the Equality Argument was offered by a Mutazilite theologian, Ibrāhīm al-Naẓẓām (d. circa 845), in his criticism of the Dahrites' account of the eternity of the world. Dahrites were a group of naturalists who denied the existence of God and believed that both the age and size of the world are infinite.[24] Although al-Naẓẓām accepts the infinite divisibility of magnitudes, he denies that time and space are infinite (by addition).[25] As reported by al-Khayyāt (d. circa 910) in *The Book of Victory* (1957, chapter 20, pp. 34–35), al-Naẓẓām's argument against the eternity of the world goes as follows: either all the stars (or celestial bodies) have the same velocity in their motions, or their velocities are different. If their velocities are different, the distances that they have traversed until now are different. Given **EI**, all these distances must be finite. This is because infinite distances must all be equal to each other. On the other hand, even if all the stars have the same velocity, the distance traversed by one star is much less than the total distance traversed by all the stars. This means again that all these distances must be finite. As it is implied by **EI**, infinite distances cannot be longer or shorter than each other. But if the distances traversed by the stars cannot be infinite, the world must have a beginning.

Interestingly, although al-Naẓẓām accepts the Equality Argument against the eternity of the world, he rejects its application against the anti-atomist view he endorsed. Among the early atomists of the Islamic world, a Plutarch–Lucretius-style argument was popular, which, roughly speaking, goes as follows: if atomism is false, then everything has an infinite number of parts. As a result, a mustard seed has the same number of parts as a mountain. But this is absurd. Therefore, atomism is true.[26] According to al-Khayyāt's report, al-Naẓẓām has

[23] For the influence of Philoponus's finitist arguments on the medieval philosophers, see, among others, Davidson (1969, 1987, chapter IV), Pines (1972), Teske (1995), and Kohler (2006).

[24] See van Ess (2017, p. 46, n. 40).

[25] Some scholars have interpreted al-Naẓẓām's view as implying that each body is actually constituted of infinitely many parts. See Pines (1997, p. 14, n. 37).

[26] In a slightly different version of this argument, it is mentioned that if atomism is false, the parts of a mustard seed (whose number is infinite) can cover the whole earth. For various versions of these arguments in the works of various Muslim thinkers, see, among others, Pines (1997, pp. 15–17) and Dhanani (1994, pp. 15–17 and 2015).

rejected this argument by claiming that although the mountain has the same number of parts, each proportion of the mountain is bigger than the same proportion of the mustard seed. Apparently, al-Naẓẓām thinks that this would suffice to save his views from the aforementioned absurdity:

T6. Al-Khayyāt (1957, *The Book of Victory*, chapter 20, p. 34)

> But as for his statement regarding the difference between the parts of a mountain and a mustard seed, Ibrāhīm [al-Naẓẓām] claims that if the mountain is halved into two halves and the mustard seed is halved into two halves, then the halves of the mountain are larger than the halves of the mustard seed. Similarly, if they are divided into quarters, fifths, or sixths, then the quarters, fifths, and sixths of the mountain are larger than those of the mustard seed. Likewise, every part of the mountain, whenever they are divided in this way, is larger than every [corresponding] part of the mustard seed, and all their parts are finite in extent and dimension.[27]

The Equality Argument is also mentioned in *A Treatise on Infinity* (1988) by Yaḥyā Ibn ʿAdī (d. 974):

T7. Ibn ʿAdī (1988, *A Treatise on Infinity*, pp. 138–39)

> The falsehood of the belief of who believes that there is an infinite thing greater than another infinite thing is clear ... [Nevertheless,] some people have thought – based on their belief that the number of days is infinite and the number of years is also infinite and it is obvious that the number of days is greater than the number of years because every year is three hundred and sixty-five days and a quarter [and is] nothing other than a fraction [of the number of days] – that they have found an infinite number that is greater than another infinite number. Also, since the individuals of any species are infinite in number, they have thought that it is possible to add to their number an infinity, which is the number of individuals of another species. So, the number of individuals of two species, while it is infinite, becomes greater than the number of individuals of a single species, which is also infinite. But it had become clear that there is no infinity in the number. And when infinity is not in it, there is no number that is infinite.

Accepting both **NIM** and **EI**, Ibn ʿAdī rejects the existence of any actual infinity and, consequently, any infinite number. In the first sentence of T7, he says that the negation of **EI** is false. He then mentions some Philoponian examples to show that if the world has no beginning, then **EI** will be false. The obvious conclusion, which is not explicitly mentioned, is that the world has a beginning.

It is noteworthy that like many other figures in the Arabic tradition, Ibn ʿAdī uses different terms for referring to *number* and *what is numbered* (i.e.,

[27] ʿAbd al-Qāhir al-Baghdādī (d. 1037), in his *The Principles of Religion* (1981, p. 36), has criticised al-Naẓẓām's response to this argument.

multitude, *collection*, or *plurality*). Referring to Aristotle's *Physics* III.5, 204b6–7, Ibn ʿAdī (1988, *A Treatise on Infinity*, p. 137) says that neither *ʿadad* (number) nor *maʿdūd* (what is numbered) can be infinite. This should leave no doubt that when he talks about the *number* of years, days, or individuals of a species in T7, what he means is not merely the multitude of those things. Rather, he talks about the number that describes how many members that multitude has. This shows that Ibn ʿAdī accepts **NIM**. In other words, he accepts that the existence of an infinite multitude implies the existence of an infinite number. However, he rejects the existence of infinite numbers because he denies that the existence of any infinite multitude is possible.[28]

Versions of the Equality Argument are discussed by Ibn Sīnā in a still unpublished treatise, 'On the Arguments of Those Who Maintain that the Past Has a Temporal Beginning', in which he critically discusses the arguments for the finitude of the past.[29] In particular, he analyses and rejects the following arguments in the fourth chapter of this treatise: (a) If the world has no beginning, both the number of things that have existed until the time of the Deluge and the number of things that have existed until our time are infinite, with the latter being greater than the former. Since this contradicts **EI**, the eternity of the world must be rejected. (b) If the world has no beginning, the existence of every individual human depends on the existence of an infinite number of their ancestors. However, something whose existence is dependent on an infinite number of things can never come into existence. So, if the world were beginningless, no individual would have existed. Since we exist now, the eternity of the world is false. More importantly, in the eighth chapter of this treatise, he argues that arguments from **EI** against the eternity of the world are unsound because **EI** applies only to the infinite multitudes or magnitudes all whose members or parts exist together. This condition of the applicability of **EI** is known as 'the wholeness condition' in the literature. A quantity S satisfies the wholeness condition if the following description is true of it:

---

28 It is worth noting that al-Rāzī's view in T1 is somewhat anticipated by Ibn ʿAdī. He argues that when we say that something is not white, our statement does not necessarily mean that that thing has a colour other than white. Our statement is true even if that thing does not have any colour at all. In the same manner, the statement that the number of something, say S, is not finite does not necessarily mean that S has a number that is infinite. Even when S has no number at all – for example, when S is not of the category of quantity – it is still true that the number of S is not finite. In the latter case, S is not finite without having an infinite number. See Ibn ʿAdī (1988, *A Treatise on Infinity*, p. 138). A very similar position is attributed to Moses Maimonides (d. 1024) by Ḥasdai Crescas (d. 1410/11). See Crescas (2018, *Light of the Lord*, Book I, Part I, chapter I, class I, p. 32).

29 For the references to the various manuscripts of this treatise, see Gutas (2014, p. 445–46). A summary of the content of this treatise is reported by Pines (1972, Appendix).

Wholeness Condition (WC): All the parts of S exist together.

According to Ibn Sīnā, it is impossible for infinities that satisfy **WC** – So sorry! It is not the most appropriate abbreviation – to be of different sizes. He thinks that no absurdity arises from the assumption that there are infinite multitudes or magnitudes of different sizes which fail to satisfy **WC**. Accordingly, no absurdity follows from that the multitude of things that have existed until our time is bigger than the multitude of things that have existed until the time of the Deluge, even if both multitudes are infinite. **EI** does not apply here. Thus, the infinitude of the past cannot be rejected through this line of argument.

Perhaps the most famous discussion of the Equality Argument in the Islamic tradition is offered by al-Ghazālī (d. 1111). In Discussion 1 of his *The Incoherence of the Philosophers*, he criticises the doctrine of the eternity of the world and offers several arguments for the finitude of the past. In particular, he presents a version of the argument from the number of revolutions of celestial bodies and then complements it with another argument which goes as follows:

T8. Al-Ghazālī (2000b, *The Incoherence of the Philosophers*, pp. 18–19)

If one were to say: 'Is the number of these revolutions even or odd, both even and odd, or neither even nor odd?', [what would you say?] If you were to say 'both even and odd or neither even nor odd', its falsity is necessarily known. If you were to say 'even', then the even becomes odd by [the addition of] a unit. How does the infinite lack a unit? And if you were to say 'odd', then the odd becomes even by [the addition of] a unit. How does that [infinity] lack the unit by the addition of which it becomes even? Thus, you have to say that it is neither even nor odd.

If it is said that 'it is only the finite that is described as even or odd and the infinite is not described as such', we say:

[You claim that there is] a collection composed of units such that it has a sixth and tenth – as previously mentioned – but it is not described as even or odd. The falsity of this is necessarily known with no reflection. With what [justification] do you disassociate yourself from this? If it is said that 'where your statement goes wrong is [where you claim] that "the collection is composed of units. However, these revolutions are non-existent. As for the past, it has ceased to exist, and as for the future, it does not [yet] exist. But the collection [must] refer to present existents. However, there is no existent here [in the collection]"', we then say:

Number is divided into the even and the odd, and it is impossible for it to lie outside this [division], regardless of whether the numbered remains or perishes. If we assume a number of horses, we must believe that it is either even or odd, regardless of whether we have supposed them to be existent or non-existent. Even if they cease to exist after existing, this matter will not change. We also have to say to them:

> According to your principle, it is not impossible to have present existents that are units varying in description while they are infinite. And [an example of] that is the human souls that are separated from bodies with death. There are existents that cannot be described as even and odd . . . This view regarding the souls is what Ibn Sīnā endorses, and it is perhaps Aristotle's doctrine.

Al-Ghazālī argues that if the world has no beginning, the number of revolutions of a celestial body is infinite and it is legitimate to ask about this number – as we can do it about any other number – whether it is even or odd. As a number, it must be either even or odd. But whether it is even or odd, only by adding one unit to it, its status changes from even to odd or vice versa. This means that there is always a lacking unit whose addition to the infinity in question can change the status of that infinity in terms of evenness and oddness. However, al-Ghazālī finds it implausible that an infinity lacks a single unit. He does not explain why he thinks so. But it is probably because of something like **EI** or the ideas that motivate it. An infinity must encompass everything, and nothing can be greater than it. Therefore, it should not be possible to change the status of an infinite multitude in terms of the evenness or oddness of the number of its members by just adding a new member to it. Accordingly, the number of the members of a multitude can be neither even nor odd. But this is not acceptable for al-Ghazālī because he thinks that every number must be either even or odd. Therefore, he denies that the number of revolutions of a celestial body can be infinite. Since the eternity of the world can grant the possibility of the infinitude of such a number, al-Ghazālī concludes that the world cannot be eternal and must have a temporal beginning.[30]

It is worth highlighting that he is so committed to **NIM** that he does not even allude to the possibility that a multitude might be infinite even if there is no infinite number that describes how many members this multitude has. Having said that, he considers the possibility that the evenness and oddness might be attributable only to finite numbers and not infinite ones. But he rejects this difference between finite numbers and the infinite number(s) in question. As it is stated in the premises of the argument from the numbers of the revolutions of celestial bodies, whether these numbers are finite or infinite, they can be multiplied and divided like other numbers. So, we can meaningfully talk about whether the number of revolutions of a star is divisible by six or ten regardless of whether or not that number is finite. Accordingly, it must also be possible to meaningfully talk about whether or not such a number is divisible by two. But this is exactly what establishes that assigning evenness and oddness to

[30] This argument is also presented in al-Ghazālī's *Moderation in Belief* (2013, pp. 37–38).

such numbers is plausible. As a result, al-Ghazālī's argument cannot be refuted by contending that evenness and oddness cannot be attributed to the infinite number of revolutions of a celestial body, or so he thinks.

Moreover, al-Ghazālī provides two reasons why the above argument from evenness and oddness cannot be refuted by appealing to **WC**. First, he insists that we can meaningfully talk about the number of things even if they do not exist. More precisely, he thinks that we can legitimately attribute numbers to the multitudes some or even all of whose members are non-existents.[31] This implies that although the past revolutions of celestial bodies do not exist now, we can meaningfully talk about the number of such revolutions and their attributes and properties. Since the above argument is about the characteristics of such numbers rather than the revolutions themselves, the non-existence of the revolutions does not jeopardise the soundness of the argument. Second, al-Ghazālī argues that even if we cannot apply the above argument to the number of the past revolutions of celestial bodies because they fail to satisfy **WC**, we can apply this argument to the number of human souls who have been separated from their bodies until now. Ibn Sīnā (to whom al-Ghazālī is objecting in T8) believes that although the human soul has a temporal origination, it will never perish after coming into existence. Thus, the souls of all the humans who have passed away so far exist now altogether. Accordingly, if the world has no temporal beginning, the multitude of human souls who are now separated from the bodies they were attached to would be an infinite multitude that satisfies **WC**. Thus, if the satisfaction of **WC** is necessary for the success of the argument from evenness and oddness, we can apply this argument to the number of existing human souls instead of the number of revolutions of a celestial body. We can, therefore, successfully refute the eternity of the world by establishing the impossibility of the infinitude of the multitude of human souls that have passed away until now through the argument from evenness and oddness, or so al-Ghazālī believes. The problem of the infinite number of human souls is also linked to the Mapping Argument against the existence of actual infinities, which will be discussed in the next section.

Variations of the Equality Argument are also defended by another Muslim theologian, Muhammad Ibn ʿAbd al-Karīm al-Shahrastānī (d. 1153). In his *Struggling with the Philosopher*, he attempts to refute the main elements of Ibn Sīnā's metaphysics by discussing five different issues, the fifth of which is the doctrine of the eternity of the world. Analysing the structure of the arguments for the finitude of the past, al-Shahrastānī identifies some of the primary

[31] This can provide another piece of evidence that he endorses **NIM**. In the fourth paragraph of T8, al-Ghazālī clearly distinguishes *number* from *numbered* and argues that we can talk about the oddness and evenness of a number, regardless of whether or not the multitude of objects it has numbered exist.

principles that can be employed in such arguments. In particular, he contends that the mere fact that something is divisible to smaller parts or fractions shows that it cannot be infinite:

T9. Al-Shahrastānī (2001, *Struggling with the Philosophers*, p. 105)

> [T]he middle term in it [i.e., an argument for finitism] is primary matters, amongst which is that the lesser in existing numbers is no equal to the greater; and amongst which is that the lesser and the greater are only [found] in the finite number, and the lesser and the greater are inconceivable to be [found] in what is infinite; and amongst which is that a determinate part – such as the half, the third, or the quarter – cannot be realised in the infinite.

He then shows how these principles can be employed to develop variations of the Equality Argument, one of which goes as follows:

T10. Al-Shahrastānī (2001, *Struggling with the Philosophers*, pp. 105–06)

> If infinitely many human souls were to exist on Sunday, then it would not be possible [for them] to increase by a number of souls on Monday. This is because what is infinite in number cannot increase by a number. But it has increased. Thus, the repetition of the negation of the consequent implies the negation of the antecedent.

The primary aim of this argument is to show that the number of human souls cannot be infinite. But a corollary of it is that the past cannot be infinite either. The argument can be reconstructed as follows: if the number of human souls that exist on Sunday is infinite, it is, in principle, possible that this number increases on Monday by new souls that come into existence on Monday. But we know that infinity cannot increase. Thus, we can conclude, by a repetitive syllogism (namely here, a *modus tollens*), that the number of souls existing on Sunday cannot be infinite at all. Since the eternity of the world confirms the possibility of the existence of an infinite number of souls by any specific day, including that specific Sunday, we have to conclude that the eternity thesis must be rejected as well.

The last principle stated in T9 implies that the multitudes of revolutions of the celestial bodies cannot be infinite because we can talk about fractions of them. For example, we saw in T5 that the number of revolutions of Saturn is a third of Jupiter's. Given this, the number of these revolutions must be finite because the infinite is indivisible and infractible, or so al-Shahrastānī thinks. Although this argument for finitism is not presented in *Struggling with the Philosophers*, a version of it can be found in al-Shahrastānī's *The End of Steps in Theology*.[32]

[32] The original Arabic title of al-Shahrastānī's book has been read in two different ways: *Nihāyat al-aqdām fī ʿilm al-kalām* (*The End of Steps in Theology*) and *Nihāyat al-iqdām fī ʿilm al-kalām* (*The Final Venture in Theology*). But as it is explained by Monnot (1996, p. 215) it seems that the

As a proponent of the doctrine of the eternity of the world, Ibn Rushd (d. 1198) – who was referred to in the Latin tradition by 'Averroes' – does not find convincing either the argument from the number of revolutions of celestial bodies or the argument from the evenness and oddness of such a number. To respond to al-Ghazālī, Ibn Rushd appeals to the fact that the rotations of a celestial body form only a *potentially* infinite multitude. He believes that although it is meaningful to talk about proportions between the actual parts of potential infinities, it does not make any sense to talk about proportions between potential infinities themselves:

T11. Ibn Rushd (1998, *The Incoherence of* The Incoherence, pp. 124–25)

If you imagine two circular movements within the two limits of the same [finite period of] time and consider a restricted part of each within the two limits of the same [finite period of] time, then the proportion of one part to the other is the same as the proportion of one whole to the other. For example, since the revolution of Saturn in a period of time that we call a year is a thirtieth of the revolution of the sun in that period, if we consider the totality of the revolutions of the sun and the totality of the revolutions of Saturn that have happened in the same period, then the proportion of the totality of the revolutions of the former motion to the totality of the revolutions of the latter motion must be the same as the proportion between their parts.

If, however, there is no proportion between the two total movements because each of them is potential – i.e., they have neither a beginning nor an end – while there is a proportion between the parts [i.e., one part of each totality] because every one of them is actual, then the proportion between one whole to the other is not necessarily the same as the proportion of one part to the other, as it is put by the group of philosophers in their reasoning. This is because there is no proportion between two magnitudes or multitudes each of which is assumed to be infinite. When the ancient assumed, for example, that the totality of the motion of the sun has no beginning or end and that the same is true of Saturn, there could be no proportion between them at all. This [is because it] (i.e., the existence of a proportion between them) entails that the two totalities are finite, as it is entailed regarding two parts of the totality.[33] And this is self-evident.[34]

Ibn Rushd seems to believe that potential infinities are not comparable to each other. Imagine that there are two rope-making machines, M_1 and M_2, such that M_1 produces one metre of rope per minute, while M_2 produces 2 metres of rope per minute. Moreover, assume they both start working now and will never stop

former reading is correct. The aforementioned version of the argument from the number of revolutions is mentioned in al-Shahrastānī (1934, p. 29). Al-Shahrastānī's view on the infinitude of the past is discussed, among others, by Mayer (2012) and Lammer (2018).

33 Given the context, the last word of this sentence should be 'totalities' rather than 'totality'.

34 Another English translation can be found in Ibn Rushd, *Averroes' Tahfut al-Tahafut* (1987, pp. 9–10).

working. Can we say that the rope that will be produced by M_1 will be twice as long as that of M_2? Ibn Rushd's answer to this question would be negative. Since the ropes that these machines will produce (if they never stop working) are potential infinities, they are not comparable to each other. These potential infinities will never have been actualised in the sense that there is no time up until which the processes of the production of such infinite ropes have been completed. This suffices to establish that the proportion between the length of the ropes that will be produced after a finite time by these two machines cannot be equal to the proportion between the total infinite ropes that these machines will produce. Indeed, such infinite ropes will never have been produced. Thus, it does not make any sense to talk about the ratio between them, or so Ibn Rushd would say. Although **EI** is, in a sense, violated here, this is not because one of these infinities is greater than the other. According to Ibn Rushd, **EI** is invalid in the case of potential infinities because they are not comparable to each other at all. Talking about the equality or inequality of potential infinities would involve a category mistake.

If the world is eternal, the multitudes of the revolutions of celestial bodies are merely potentially infinite. Thus, we cannot compare them to each other and meaningfully talk about their halves, thirds, or other fractions. Therefore, the finitist arguments from the revolutions of celestial bodies and from evenness and oddness fail. This seems to be what Ibn Rushd wants to convey by T11. Nevertheless, it is still unclear why Ibn Rushd assumes that potential infinities are not comparable to each other. One might think this is because potential infinities fail to satisfy **WC**. For example, one might read Ibn Rushd as saying that the infinite multitude of the revolutions of Saturn is incomparable to the infinite multitude of the revolutions of the sun because these multitudes fail to satisfy **WC**. However, if the comparability of two multitudes hinges on the satisfaction of **WC**, then even the finite fractions of those two multitudes are not comparable to each other. For example, **WC** is not satisfied either by the multitude of the revolutions of Saturn in the last three years or by the multitude of the revolutions of the sun in the same period. Thus, we should conclude that these finite multitudes are incomparable to each other because they fail to satisfy **WC**. Even worse, revolutions do not happen instantaneously. Thus, no revolution exists as a whole at any moment of (the past, present, or future) time. Accordingly, if we accept that only the present is real and only the present things exist, as Ibn Rushd and most of the medieval thinkers mentioned in this Element do, then no revolution—let alone any multitude of revolutions—satisfies WC. This implies that the multitudes of revolutions, whether finite or infinite, are not comparable to each other at all. But this does not seem a desirable consequence for Ibn Rushd. Unfortunately, he has not provided any more helpful explanation on how this undesirable result can be avoided.

A more abstract version of the Equality Argument goes as follows: assume that there is an infinite whole. Remove a finite part from it. What remains must be infinite. Otherwise, the initial whole is composed of two finite parts and must be finite. As a result, every infinite whole has infinite parts. However, given **CN5**, every whole is greater than its parts. Thus, if there are infinite wholes, there are infinities some of which are greater than others. This contradicts **EI**. Accordingly, the assumption of the existence of infinite wholes must be rejected. Arguments of this level of abstraction are presented by the Jewish philosopher, Bachya Ben Joseph Ibn Paquda (d. 1120) – whose Arabic name is 'Baḥy Ibn Yūsuf Ibn Bāqūda – in his *Duties of the Heart* (1996, Gate 1, chapter 5, 82–85). A geometrical version of such arguments is presented by Ibn Bājja (d. 1138) – who was referred to in the Latin tradition by 'Avempace' – in his *Commentary on Aristotle's* Physics (1991, Book III, p. 38): suppose that there is an infinite line AB that starts from A and extends infinitely in the direction of B. Moreover, suppose that AC is an initial final segment of AB. On the one hand, CB is a part of AB. Therefore, **CN5** implies that AB is greater than CB. On the other hand, CB must be infinite. Otherwise, AB – which is composed of AC and CB – would also be finite. But if AB and CB are both infinite, then we have two infinities, one greater than the other. This contradicts **EI**. As a result, the initial assumption that AC is infinite must be rejected. There is no infinite magnitude (Fig. 2).[35]

Ibn Bājja (1991, *Commentary on Aristotle's* Physics, Book III, p. 40) believes this argument only establishes the impossibility of the magnitudes that satisfy **WC**. That is why it cannot be employed to reject the infinitude of the past. Following Ibn Sīnā, Ibn Bājja contends that since the line of time fails to satisfy **WC**, the infinity of time is immune to the arguments for finitism.

Another interesting point that Ibn Bājja makes is about the compatibility of finitism with the methodology of mathematical sciences. Following Aristotle (*Physics* III.7, 207b28–38), Ibn Bājja says:

> T12. Ibn Bājja (1991, *Commentary on Aristotle's* Physics, Book III, p. 40)
>
> Mathematical sciences do not employ infinity, except when an extending magnitude is hypothesised [and] it is [assumed that it is] possible to take a [magnitude] larger than it. They [i.e., mathematical sciences] do not need

Figure 2 The existence of infinite lines can be rejected by the conjunction of **CN5** and **EI**.

[35] Many other scholars have mentioned this geometrical argument in their works. Notably, a discussion of it can be found in al-Shahrastānī's *The End of Steps in Theology* (1934, p. 13).

> the existence of the infinite in actuality and perfection; they only need it in potentiality and possibility.

Ibn Bājja contends that actual infinities are not needed even for purely mathematical purposes. He seems to think that arguments for finitism apply to magnitudes and multitudes even if we take them to be merely mental (or mind-dependent) existents.[36] He explicitly claims that 'it is impossible for estimation (*wahm*) to present [the parts of an] infinity actually altogether'. Given that, in the context of the post-Avicennian Islamic philosophy, 'estimation' refers to the cognitive faculty which enables us to entertain fictional and imaginary objects and/or scenarios, Ibn Bājja must be interpreted as saying that the parts of an infinity cannot coexist even in mind and as purely mental existents. Put differently, Ibn Bājja believes that there is no infinity that satisfies **WC** even if the notion of EXISTENCE mentioned in **WC** is taken to be merely MENTAL EXISTENCE. His position must be understood in contrast with the views of people who believe that arguments for finitism establish the impossibility of an infinity only if it satisfies a condition that I call 'the extramental existence condition'. A quantity S satisfies this condition if the following description is true of it:

Extramental Existence Condition (EEC): All the parts of S exist extramentally (or mind-independently).

Note that **WC** and **EEC** are independent of each other in the sense that a quantity might satisfy neither, both, or only one of these conditions. Ibn Bājja believes that the Equality Argument establishes the impossibility of any infinity that fulfils **WC** regardless of whether or not it also fulfils **EEC**. This condition also plays a crucial role in discussions of the Mapping Argument that is the subject of the next section.

The eminent Jewish philosopher, Moses Maimonides (d. 1204) – whose Arabic name is 'Mūsa Ibn Maymūn' – has mentioned the arguments from the revolutions of celestial bodies and from the number of human souls in his presentation of the anti-eternity views of the Muslim theologians in *The Guide of the Perplexed* (1967, I.74, p. 222). Although Maimonides thinks these arguments are not compelling, he does not specify where exactly they go wrong. But this does not undermine the significance of *The Guide of the*

[36] A criticism of this view is offered by Gersonides (d. 1344) in his discussion of Ibn Rushd's mathematical finitism. See Kohler (2006, section III). Endorsing this sort of mathematical finitism was a prevalent position among those medieval philosophers who considered mathematical objects as properties of existing physical objects. To give an example from the Latin tradition, Thomas Aquinas (d. 1274) – who defends such a realist ontology of mathematics – argues, in his *Summa Theologiae* (2006, Ia. 7, 3, p. 103), that 'Geometers need not postulate lines which are actually infinite, but lines from which they can cut off whatever length they require, and such are the lines they call infinite'. For a recent work on Aquinas's ontology of mathematics, see Rioux (2023).

Perplexed in the history of the idea of infinities of different sizes. This book was translated first from Arabic into Hebrew and then from Hebrew into Latin in the thirteenth century. The Latin translation, which was entitled *Dux neutrorum*, was completed around 1220–1240. It might be through *Dux neutrorum* that the Equality Argument was transmitted into the Latin tradition. *Dux neutrorum* is likely to be one of the sources of William of Auvergne (d. 1249), the first Latin author (or, at least, one of the first ones) who offered arguments for the finitude of the past.[37] These arguments are presented in his *The Universe of Creatures,* and some of them are in the style of the Equality Argument. According to one of these arguments, for each revolution of the sun, there are 360 degrees of the motion of the sun, and each degree of this motion is equal to one day. Therefore, for each revolution of the sun, there are 360 days. This establishes that if the world has no beginning, there are two infinities one of them 360 times greater than the other. Since this contradicts **EI**, the doctrine of eternity must be rejected (William of Auvergne 1998, *The Universe of Creatures*, p. 137). William of Auvergne also presents another argument that is exclusively about the definite proportions between the revolutions of celestial bodies. Discussing the proportions between the revolutions of a few celestial bodies (e.g., Saturn, Jupiter, the sun, etc.), he concludes that 'the revolutions of each of the planets will be according to astronomical calculation a definite part, that is, will have a definite proportion to all the revolutions of the heaven taken together, which are completed in the whole of time, which comes to an end in the present moment. It is impossible, however, that it be infinite since its parts are found to have a definite relation and proportion to it, etc.' (William of Auvergne 1998, *The Universe of Creatures*, p. 138). This means that if the world is eternal, then the multitude of the revolutions of each celestial body is a definite proportion of the multitude of all the revolutions happening in the heaven, while both of these multitudes are infinite. This, again, is incompatible with **EI**, given that the aforementioned proportion is not the ratio of 1 to 1.[38] Thus, the world must have a beginning. Both of these arguments rely on observations about the actual state of the world. However, before these arguments, another argument is presented by William that appeals to our intuitions about counterfactual but still imaginable states of the world. That argument goes as follows:

[37] On the sources of William of Auvergne for the Equality Argument, see Mancosu (forthcoming, section 3.1).

[38] The fact that the aforementioned proportion is not the ratio of 1 to 1 can be concluded from **CN5**. The multitude of the revolutions of each celestial body is a proper part of the multitude of all the revolutions happening in the heaven. **CN5** implies that the latter multitude is greater than the former. Accordingly, the ratio between their sizes is not 1 to 1.

T13. William of Auvergne (1998, *The Universe of Creatures*, pp. 137)

> But if he [i.e., Aristotle] says that the heaven completed an infinite number of revolutions in the whole of past time, I shall imagine – for this imagining is possible for the intellect – that the heaven moved in the whole of past time by a velocity that was less by half. Because, then, the proportion of the one motion to the other is the same as the proportion of amount traversed to the other amount traversed, it is necessarily the case that in the same time it completed only a half of the number of revolutions. The revolutions, then, which it completed in the whole of past time, necessarily have a half, and in the same way they have a quarter and an eighth and so on to infinity. But it is evident that the infinite does not have a half.
>
> Moreover, when the opposite is imagined, namely, that the motion of the whole heaven in the whole time that has passed is twice as fast, then, for the same reason the revolutions completed in the same time will be twice as many. But the heaven will not complete more revolutions than those which have passed and those which are in the future taken together, but it completed that number by having revolved at twice the speed; hence, it has completed its motion.
>
> Moreover, there is no doubt that it would have completed twice as many revolutions if its velocity was doubled, and would have done so in the same time. Hence, the number of revolutions already completed had a double, and it is the half of some number. Such a number, therefore, is not infinite, since it has a half, as was said, and also a double.[39]

Assume that the heaven is rotating with velocity v. Furthermore, assume that the world has no beginning and the number of the past revolutions of the heaven is I. However, the heaven could have a different velocity. But if the velocity of the motion of the heaven were different, the number of its revolutions would have been proportionally different. For example, if the velocity of this motion were $v/2$, then the number of revolutions would have been $I/2$. Generally, it is conceivable that the heaven has velocity $v/2^n$ for some $n \geq 1$. But if the velocity were $v/2^n$, the number of revolutions would have been $I/2^n$. Thus, I has a half, a quarter, etc. This establishes that I cannot be infinite. This is because infinity does not have a half, a quarter, and so on. On the other hand, if I is a finite number, then the world must have a beginning. In the last two paragraphs of T13, the same argument is repeated by velocities $2^n v$ $(n \geq 1)$, which would change the number of revolutions of the heaven to $2^n I$. As a result, I has also a double, a quadruple, and so on. The incompatibility of this result with **EI** affirms, once again, the finitude of I and the finitude of the past, or so William of Auvergne contends.[40]

[39] The square brackets are mine.

[40] For more details about William of Auvergne's arguments for that the universe has a beginning, see Teske (1990, 1995, and 2000).

The Equality Argument can be found in many later medieval Latin texts. For example, in a commentary on the *Sentences* of Peter Lombard (d. 1160), Bonaventure (d. 1274) mentioned a version of the argument from the number of revolutions of celestial bodies to reject the beginninglessness of the world (1882, *Commentary on the Sentences*, Book II, Distinction 1, Part 1, Article 1, Question 2). Bonaventure (1964, *On the Eternity of the World*, p. 108) makes it explicit that this argument is based on one of the '*per se* known propositions of reason and philosophy' that states that 'it is impossible to add to the infinite'. Murdoch (1981, p. 52) believes that it was probably the inclusion of this argument in Bonaventure's 'examination of the possibility of an eternal world that gave it the status of a *sine qua non* element in almost all subsequent discussions of this controversial problem' (see also Murdoch 1982, pp. 569–70).[41] According to Bonaventure (1964, *On the Eternity of the World*, p. 109–10), another *per se* known proposition that can be taken as a ground for arguments against the eternity of the world states that 'it is impossible that there be simultaneously an infinite number of things'. To use the terminology introduced earlier, this proposition can be read as saying that 'no infinity that satisfies **WC** can be realised'. Bonaventure then argues that the eternity of the world is in tension with this principle because it implies the existence of an infinity of human souls that simultaneously exist.

As another example of the Latin discussions of the Equality Argument, it is interesting to see a slightly different construction that still relies on the principles mentioned in the previous versions we saw. Roger Bacon, in his *Opus Tertium* (2012, pp. 141–42), develops an argument whose core idea can be simplified as follows: consider a straight line that is infinitely extended in directions DC. Moreover, assume that A and B are two points existing on DC so that, compared to B, A is closer to C (Fig. 3).

Figure 3 A visualisation of Bacon's version of the Equality Argument.

[41] In a brief note, Brown (1965) has interpreted Bonaventure's argument as stating that if the past was infinite, then the infinite set of the revolutions of the moon could be put in a one-to-one correspondence with a proper subset of it. However, I think this interpretation is not tenable. The discussion of one-to-one correspondence appears in a different type of medieval arguments for finitism that will be discussed in the next section.

Now, consider the following line of argument:

(1) AD = AC. This is because they are both infinite and **EI** is true.
(2) BC = BD. This is because they are both infinite and **EI** is true.
(3) BC > AC. This is because AC is a part of BC and **CN5** is true.
(4) BC > AD. This is true because of (1) and (3).
(5) BD > AD. This is true because of (2) and (4)
(6) BD < AD. This is because BD is a part of AD and **CN5** is true.
(7) BD > AD and BD < AD. This is true because of (5) and (6).

But (7) expresses a contradiction. This means that the initial assumption of the existence of an infinite line extended in both directions is implausible. What Bacon concludes from this is that the size of the world cannot be infinite. The infinitude of the world's size implies the existence of one-dimensional magnitudes infinitely extended in both directions. But the above proof reveals that the existence of such magnitudes is absurd.[42]

Versions of the Equality Argument have been criticised not only by philosophers who accepted the existence of actual infinities but also by philosophers who affirm that no actual infinity exists. As an example of the former group of philosophers, we can mention Henry of Harclay (d. 1317), who criticised the arguments for the finitude of the past from the number of revolutions of celestial bodies and defended the idea of the existence of actual infinities.[43] By contrast, Naṣīr al-Dīn al-Ṭūsī (d. 1274) is one of those philosophers who cast doubt on the validity of such arguments against the eternity of the world without accepting the existence of actual infinities. He believes that although the past (or, more particularly, the multitude of the past revolutions of a celestial body) is infinite, its infinitude does not imply any absurdity. In his *The Wrestlings Down of the Wrestler*, al-Ṭūsī responds to al-Shahrastānī's criticisms of Ibn Sīnā's view regarding the eternity of the world by explicitly accepting that infinities which fail to satisfy **WC** can, in principle, be of different sizes. Such infinities can be divided into smaller parts that are themselves infinite. They can also be added to or multiplied. Put differently, al-Ṭūsī believes that **EI** does not apply to infinities whose parts fail to exist altogether. One such infinity can be greater or smaller than another, and this does not lead to any implausible consequences (al-Ṭūsī 2004, *The Wrestlings Down of the Wrestler*, pp. 183–85).

The Equality Argument has been addressed in many other texts that we cannot investigate here due to space constraints. Nevertheless, what we saw in this section from the long history of this argument and its miscellaneous

[42] For a reconstruction of this argument that is more faithful to Bacon's original presentation of it, see Mancosu (forthcoming, section 4.1.1). In the same chapter, Mancosu discusses arguments of the same spirit by John Peckham (d. 1292) and Peter John Olivi (d. 1298).

[43] See, among others, Sylla (2021, p. 63).

versions suffices to reveal both its significance in the historical evolution of our conception of infinities of different sizes and its naivety and shortcomings. It was probably through the Equality Argument that the attention of the philosophers was drawn for the first time in history to the fact that the existence of an infinity could imply the existence of other infinities that might or might not be of the same size. Admittedly, no clear and explicit definition of *size* as it applies to infinities is offered in the context of discussions regarding this argument. The advocates of this argument take **EI** for granted without introducing any sufficient criterion for the *equality* of infinities. Nevertheless, it appears that they appeal to **CN5** as a sufficient criterion for the *inequality* of infinities. Accordingly, the gist of the argument is to establish a tension between (a) the existence of unequal infinities, which follows from the conjunction of **CN5** and the assumption of the existence of an infinity and (b) the equality of all infinities – that is, **EI** – that is taken for granted with no sufficient criterion for equality. One step forward towards a more accurate understanding of the possibility of the existence of infinities of different sizes is to introduce a sufficient criterion for the equality of infinities. This is precisely what has been done in the Mapping Argument.

4 The Mapping Argument

Another principle widely employed in medieval discussions of infinity is the fourth common notion from the first book of Euclid's *The Elements* (1908, vol. 1, p. 155). This common notion, usually known as the Axiom of Congruence, states that 'things which coincide with one another are equal to one another' ('τὰ ἐφαρμόζοντα ἐπ' ἀλλήλα ἴσα ἀλλήλοις ἐστίν'). The term 'ἐφαρμόζοντα' comes from the Greek verb 'ἐφαρμόζειν'. Although the translation of 'ἐφαρμόζειν' to 'to coincide' (or 'to correspond') is not incorrect, it does not reflect the exact (or complete) meaning of this verb in the geometrical contexts in which Euclid employs the aforementioned common notion. He has appealed to this common notion in the proofs of some theorems (e.g., I.4, I.8, and III.24) to conclude certain equalities from coincidences or correspondences realised as a result of superposing or mapping some geometrical figures upon others. Thus, 'ἐφαρμόζειν' expresses a particular sort of coincidence or correspondence which occurs as a result of the application of a specific method of the comparison of quantities (i.e., the mapping or superposition technique). This sense of ἐφαρμόζειν is better captured in the later Arabic and Latin translations of *The Element*. For example, in the so-called Isḥāq-Thābit translation, this common notion is rendered as 'things none of which exceeds another – whenever one of them is mapped [or superposed] on another – are equal'.[44] This construal of the fourth Euclidean common notion, which can be expressed more simply as follows, plays a crucial role in the development of medieval theories of infinity:

Common Notion 4 (CN4): If one thing is mapped/superposed upon another thing and neither exceeds the other, the two things are equal to each other.

CN4 has been used both in certain theories about infinitely large quantities originating from the Islamic–Arabic tradition and in certain theories about infinitely small quantities originating from the Christian–Latin tradition. The central notion in both groups of theories is the same notion that can be expressed by 'ἐφαρμόζειν' in Greek. This notion is associated with the Arabic '*inṭibāq*' or '*taṭbīq*' in the former theories about infinitely large quantities and with the Latin 'superponere' in the latter theories about infinitely small quantities. To highlight the different functions of the notions expressed by these terms, I prefer to translate them into different English terms. Accordingly, I translate '*inṭibāq*' and 'superponere' as, respectively, 'to map' and 'to superpose' in English.[45] However, it must be noted that in many (though not all) of the following discussions of finitism, these two verbs can be used interchangeably.

CN4 has been employed with **CN5** in one of the most famous medieval arguments for finitism, usually called 'the Mapping Argument'. The core idea behind this argument goes as follows: if an infinity exists, it can be shown, by appealing to **CN4**, that it would be equal to some of its parts. But this contradicts **CN5**. Therefore, no infinity exists. This general line of thought has been qualified in different versions of the Mapping Argument. Probably, the earliest version of this argument is presented by al-Kindī.[46] He believes that this argument shows that every quantity must be finite. This implies that space (or, more specifically, the size of the world) and time (or, more specifically, the age

44 The Isḥāq-Thābit translation is the second Arabic translation of *The Elements*. This translation was made by Isḥāq Ibn Ḥunayn (d. circa 910) and revised by Thābit Ibn Qurra al-Ḥarrānī (d. 901). A copy of this translation can be found in the codex 6581/1 of the Majlis Library in Tehran. The fourth common notion is mentioned in folio 2a, ll. 4–5. The first Arabic translation of *The Element* was made by al-Ḥajjāj Ibn Yūsuf Ibn Maṭar (d. 833) and was later revised by himself. Neither of the two versions of al-Ḥajjāj's translation is extant today. His translation was the source of the first Latin translation of *The Elements* by Adelard of Bath (d. 1152?). The formulation of the fourth Euclidean common notion in Adelard's translation is almost the same as in the Isḥāq-Thābit translation. Adelard has translated 'ἐφαρμόζειν' as 'superponere'. See Busard (1983, p. 33, ll. 80–81).

45 On the pivotal role of the notion of SUPERPOSITION in the medieval Latin theories of infinitesimals and continuity, see Murdoch (1964).

46 This argument has been presented in al-Kindī's *On First Philosophy* (2012, pp. 20–21) and three short treatises on the finitude of the past (2012, pp. 60–73). Al-Kindī's account of infinity has been discussed, among others, by Rescher and Khatchadourian (1965), Shamsi (1975), Adamson (2007, chapter 4), and Abdel Meguid (2018).

of the world) must be finite. But this is compatible with the possibility of the expansion of the world with no limit over time and with the endlessness of the future. Thus, the size and age of the world can be potentially infinite but not actually infinite, or so al-Kindī (2012, *On First Philosophy*, pp. 21–22) believes. Ibn Sīnā rehabilitated al-Kindī's argument, and the Avicennian version of the Mapping Argument became popular among medieval thinkers. He has presented this argument with slight differences in several works.[47] The version offered in *The Physics of* The Healing goes as follows:

T14. Ibn Sīnā (2009, *The Physics of* The Healing, chapter III.8, § 1)

> It is impossible that a magnitude (*miqdār*), number, or [multitude of] numbered things (*ma ʿdūdāt*) having an order (*tartīb*) either in nature (*al-ṭab ʿ*) or in position (*al-waḍ ʿ*) is instantiated as an actual existent with no end [i.e., as an infinite actual existent]. That is because for every infinite magnitude and every infinite [multitude of] numbered things possessing an order, their extension towards an actual infinity is either in [all of] their directions or in a single direction. If [their infinitude] is in all of their directions, then let us posit a limit within it – such as a point in a line, or a line in a surface, or a surface in a body, or a unit in a numeric totality – and make it a limit. So, we will talk about it inasmuch as we define it as a limit. [Call this limiting point A.] Now, we take a finite part – say AC – from AB, which is infinite in the direction of B. So, if [something] equal to CB were mapped upon or laid parallel to AB or some [other appropriate] relation between them is considered, then either it [i.e., CB] will extend infinitely in the same direction as AB, or it [i.e., CB] will fall short of AB by an [amount] equal to AC. Now, if AB corresponds (*muṭābaqan*) to CB [as they are extending] to infinity, while CB is a part of AB, then the whole and the portion correspond [to each other]. This is a contradiction. If CB falls short of AB in the direction of B and is less than it, then CB is finite, and AB exceeds it by the finite [amount] AC. Therefore, AB is finite. It was, however, [supposed to be] infinite. So, it becomes evidently clear from this [discussion] that the existence of an actual infinity among ordered numbers and magnitudes is impossible.

Assume that there exists an infinite one-dimensional magnitude – that is, an infinite straight line – AB starting from point A and extending infinitely in the direction of B. Remove a finite part AC from its beginning, and map the remaining part – that is, CB or, more precisely, a copy of it, say C*B* – upon AC so that C* is positioned in front of A and the two lines are parallel to each other. If C*B* falls short of AC, then C*B* and, consequently, CB would be finite (Fig. 4a). Since AC is finite by assumption, AB, which is composed of two finite parts, must also be finite. However, this contradicts the initial assumption

[47] Zarepour (forthcoming) investigates the evolution of Ibn Sīnā's view regarding the exact structure, purpose, and applicability conditions of the Mapping Argument over the course of his career.

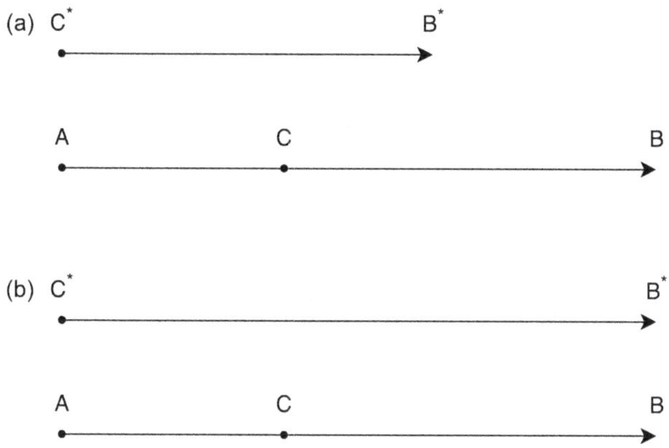

Figure 4 A visualisation of the Mapping Argument against the existence of infinite magnitudes.

of the infinitude of AC. Thus, C*B* does not fall short of AC. But if the two lines correspond to (or coincide with) each other so that neither exceeds the other, then **CN4** implies that they are equal to each other (Fig. 4b). This means that AB equals C*B* and, consequently, CB. But CB is a part of AB. Accordingly, **CN5** implies that AB must be greater than (CB). They cannot be equal to each other. Thus, we have a contradiction. This establishes that we have to reject the initial assumption we started from, that is, the existence of an infinite one-dimensional magnitude.

In this version of the Mapping Argument, the notion of MAPPING must be understood as the superposition of a geometrical figure upon another. If the two figures cover each other so that no part of any of them remains uncovered by the other, then the two figures coincide with and are equal to each other in the sense of **CN4**. Although this sense of mapping applies to magnitudes, it does not seem to apply to multitudes. That is why the version of the Mapping Argument presented in T14 appears to be inapplicable to numbers and multitudes of objects, even though T14 explicitly rejects the actual existence of not only infinite magnitudes but also infinite numbers and infinite multitudes of numbered things (albeit if they satisfy certain conditions). Of course, as shown in Books 7–9 of *The Elements*, numbers can be represented as magnitudes. As a result, any argument against the existence of infinite magnitudes can also be taken as an argument against the existence of infinite numbers.[48] Nevertheless,

[48] Maimonides has listed twenty-five premises for the proof of the existence of God at the beginning of *The Guide of the Perplexed* (1963, pp. 235–40). Muḥammad al-Tabrīzī (d. 13th century), a thirteenth-century Persian Muslim scholar, has written a commentary in Arabic on these premises. This work, which was probably the first commentary on a part of *The Guide*, was

the version of the Mapping Argument mentioned in T14 – which I call 'the magnitude version' – does not itself directly apply to discrete quantities and, in particular, to the multitudes of objects. Ibn Sīnā was apparently aware that there is another version of the Mapping Argument that directly applies to multitudes. Nonetheless, he never explicitly mentioned this version – which I call 'the multitude version' – in his works. The multitude version of the Mapping Argument is presented in the works of his commentators and critics. For example, al-Shahrastānī proposes an example of the multitude version of the Mapping Argument in his *Struggling with the Philosopher* to establish that the chain of the ancestors of a person cannot be infinite. Analysing the magnitude version of the Mapping Argument, he contends that, in the application of the mapping technique, we need to 'map the point on the point and the line on the line' (al-Shahrastānī, 2001, *Struggling with the Philosopher*, p. 108). Apparently, what he has in mind here is the one-to-one correspondence of the points or equally long segments of the two lines, one of which is mapped upon the other. He believes that we can 'apply this argument as it is to the numbers of human souls and the numbers of circular motion [of celestial bodies]' (al-Shahrastānī, 2001, *Struggling with the Philosopher*, p. 108). Regarding the former, he proposes the following argument for the finitude of the chain of the ancestors of any given human being:

> T15. Al-Shahrastānī (2001, *Struggling with the Philosophers*, p. 109)
>
> Hypothesise Zayd and consider him as a point; and hypothesise his forefathers to infinity [as points on] a straight line. Also, hypothesise ʿAmr and consider him as a point falling short of Zayd with one forefather or two forefathers or three; and consider his ancestors to infinity as a line. Moreover, suppose that Zayd and ʿAmr are twins in existence, and carry the argument to its conclusion.

The argument could have been presented in a more precise form. Nonetheless, the exact content that is supposed to be conveyed is not hard to guess: assume that the chain of the ancestors of any given human being is infinite. Therefore,

translated into Hebrew by Isaac ben Nathan of Cordoba (d. 14th century) and used as a primary source by Ḥasdai Crescas in many of the discussions of his *Light of the Lord* (2018). The first of those premises rejects the existence of infinite magnitudes, and the second denies the existence of infinite multitudes of bodies that satisfy **WC**. To justify the second premise, al-Tabrīzī appeals to the first premise and argues that no such multitude exists because otherwise an infinite magnitude will exist. More importantly, to justify the first premise, he presents a version of the mapping argument in which the infinite magnitude in question is assumed to be constituted of consecutive segments of equal lengths. See al-Tabrīzī (1981, *Commentary on the Twenty-Five Premises for the Proof of the Existence of God*, pp. 7–8 and 17). For Crescas's presentation of the Mapping Argument, see Wolfson (1929, pp. 346–47) and Crescas (2018, p. 37).

the following multitudes are infinite: (a) the multitude of Zayd, his father, the father of his father, the father of the father of his father, and so on ad infinitum; and (b) the multitude of ʿAmr, his father, the father of his father, the father of the father of his father, and so on ad infinitum. If we assume that ʿAmr himself is one of the forefathers of Zayd and, accordingly, a member of (a), then (b) would be a part of (a). Moreover, we can suppose that the human beings in (a) are points with equal successive distances from each other on a straight line starting from a point corresponding to Zayd and extending infinitely. Part of this line is a line that starts from a point corresponding to ʿAmr and extends in the same manner as (a). Now, we can map the line corresponding to (b) on the line corresponding to (a) so that the point corresponding to ʿAmr is mapped upon the point corresponding to Zayd. To make this process of mapping more easily imaginable, al-Shahrastānī suggests that we can take ʿAmr as the twin of Zayd (and any ancestor of ʿAmr as the twin of the corresponding ancestor of Zayd). Of course, this does not mean that ʿAmr is both an ancestor and the twin of Zayd. Al-Shahrastānī just wants to reassure his readers that the mapping process can be completed and every member of (a) can be paired with a member of (a copy of) (b) in the same manner as twins (Fig. 5). If (a) is infinite, then (b) would be infinite too. Moreover, the completion of the mapping process establishes that (a) and (b) are equal due to **CN4**. However, this result is incompatible with **CN5** because (b) is a part of (a). Thus, the infinitude of (a) and, consequently, (b) must be rejected.

A more abstract example of the application of the multitude version of the Mapping Argument is presented in Fakhr al-Dīn al-Rāzī's commentary on Ibn Sīnā's *Fountains of Wisdom*. In his commentary, after discussing a version of the Mapping Argument that is presented in the *Physics* part of *Fountains of Wisdom*, al-Rāzī anticipates twelve objections to this argument and tries to rebut them. In the eleventh objection, he says that one might reject the Mapping

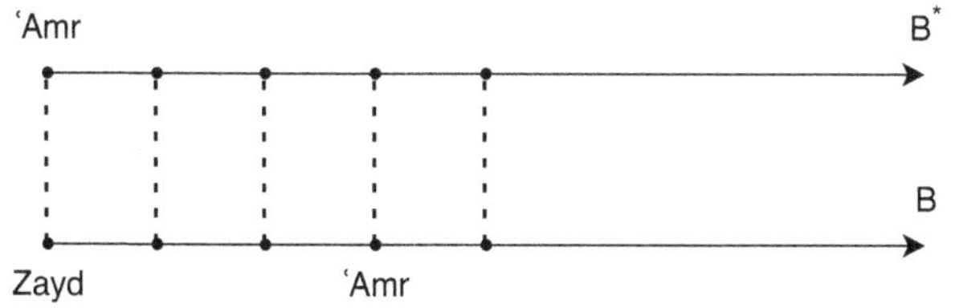

Figure 5 An application of the multitude version of the Mapping Argument to show that the chain of the ancestors of a human being cannot be infinite.

Argument because it implies the unacceptable consequence that even the multitude of all natural numbers must be finite:

> T16. Al-Rāzī (1994, *Commentary on* Fountains of Wisdom, vol. 2, p. 53)
>
> Let's take the [multitude that includes every] number from one to what has no end in terms of the ranks of additions together with another multitude [that includes every number other than a few initial numbers]. We put the first rank of this [latter] multitude in front of the first rank of that [former] multitude, and the second of this in front of the second of that, and so on successively. So, if the remainder does not appear [i.e., if by following this procedure nothing of the latter multitudes remains unpaired], then the more is identical to the less. And, if the remainder appears at the end of the ranks [of the former multitude, and some ranks of the latter multitude remains unpaired], then it entails the finitude of number in the direction of its increase; and it is self-evident for the intellect that this is impossible.

In the multitude version of the Mapping Argument, mapping a multitude upon another is nothing but putting their members into one-to-one correspondence by pairing each member of one multitude with one and only one member of the other. According to this argument, some proper submultitudes of any infinite multitude can be mapped upon it so that no member of any of them remains unpaired. Coupling this with **CN4**, we can conclude that every infinite multitude is, in a sense, equal to some of its proper submultitude. But this is incompatible with **CN5**, according to which every multitude is greater than (and, therefore, not equal to) any of its proper submultitudes. Thus, the existence of infinite multitudes is impossible.

T16 objects to this line of reasoning. On the one hand, it is undeniable that the multitude of all natural numbers is infinite. On the other hand, if we apply the multitude version of the Mapping Argument to this multitude, we can show that it is equal to some of its proper submultitudes. For example, by employing **CN4** and pairing 1 with 11, 2 with 12, 3 with 13, and n with n+10 in general, we can show that the multitude of all natural numbers is quantitatively equal (or, as it is usually said in modern set theory, equinumerous) to the multitude of the natural numbers greater than 10 (Fig. 6).[49] But the latter multitude is a proper

[49] Note a significant difference between the two versions of the Mapping Argument presented in T15 and T16: in the former text, the members of the multitudes in question are imagined as points with equal successive distances from each other on straight lines. The points on one line are then paired with those of the other by superposing one of the two lines upon the other. However, the argument developed in T16 is free from such an assumption. The numbers in one multitude are paired with those of the other by successively putting them in front of each other. Nevertheless, these numbers are not assumed to be lined up with equal distances from each other on straight lines. The superposition of lines does not play any role in the latter version of the Mapping Argument. In this sense, compared to T15, what we see in T16 is closer to a general notion of ONE-TO-ONE CORRESPONDENCE.

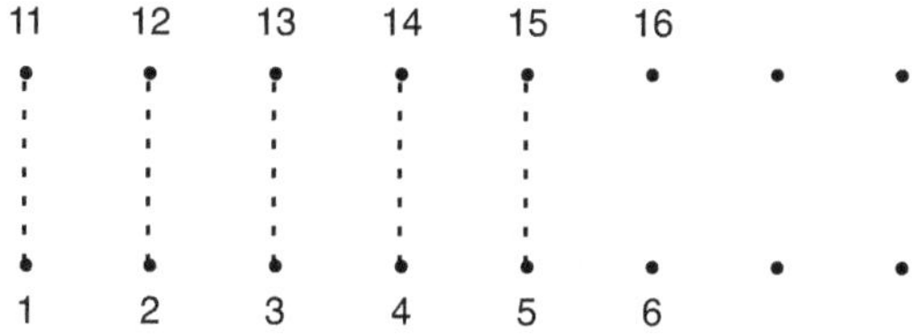

Figure 6 One-to-one correspondence between the multitude of all natural numbers and the multitude of all natural numbers greater than 10.

submultitude of the former. Thus, if we endorse **CN5**, a contradiction follows. Accordingly, the existence of the infinite multitude of natural numbers must be denied.

Before discussing al-Rāzī's response to this objection, we should see what conditions Ibn Sīnā considers for the applicability of the Mapping Argument. In his presentations of the Mapping Argument in various places of his oeuvre, Ibn Sīnā consistently insists that this argument rejects the actual existence of the infinities that are or can be ordered. Put differently, the aim of the original version of the Mapping Argument presented by Ibn Sīnā is to establish the impossibility of any infinity that satisfies two conditions. One of these conditions concerns the actuality of the infinity in question, while the other concerns its orderedness. To be more specific, this argument cannot establish the impossibility of potential infinities. Putting together his discussions of this condition in various places of his works, we can conclude that what he means by the actual existence of an infinity is nothing but the fulfilment of **WC** – that is the simultaneous existence of all the parts of the infinity in question. In other words, he believes that the Mapping Argument cannot establish the impossibility of an infinity that fails to satisfy **WC**.

Ibn Sīnā does not explain why the satisfaction of **WC** is necessary for the applicability of the Mapping Argument. But what he had in mind is probably that if all the parts of S are not supposed to exist together simultaneously, then it does not make any sense to talk about whether or not S as a whole can be equal to some of its parts. On this interpretation, **CN5** does not express a logical fact about any whole regardless of its nature. In particular, if it is legitimate to talk about wholes that are cross-temporal mereological sums of elements that do not exist simultaneously, then **CN5** is not true of such wholes. As a result, the infinitude of such wholes cannot be rendered impossible by appealing to an argument which, like the Mapping Argument, relies on **CN5**. That is why, at the end of his discussion of the Mapping Argument in *The Salvation* (1985, chapter IV.2, pp. 245–46), Ibn Sīnā contends that this argument cannot establish the finitude of time. By contrast, al-Kindī did not believe that the applicability of (his own version of) this argument hinges on the satisfaction of a condition like **WC**. That is why he had no hesitation in rejecting the infinitude of the past by applying this argument to the past time.

In addition to **WC**, Ibn Sīnā considers another condition for the applicability of the Mapping Argument, which concerns the notion of ORDER. He believes that the mapping technique does not apply to an infinity whose parts are not ordered either in nature or in position (see, e.g., the first sentence of T14). Unfortunately, it is not crystal clear what he means by order in nature or position. Thus, looking at the origins of the discussion of *order among the parts of a quantity* might be beneficial. Aristotle contends that 'some [quantities] are composed of parts which have position in relation to one another, others are not composed of parts which have position' (*Categories* 6, 4b21–25). To provide examples of the former type of quantities, he mentions line and plane because each part of them is situated somewhere. These parts can be distinguished by where they are situated. Regarding these parts, 'one could say where each is situated and which join on to one another' (*Categories* 6, 5a21–22). By contrast, one cannot say regarding the parts of things like number and time that they 'have some position in relation to one another or are situated somewhere, nor see which of the parts join on to one another' (*Categories* 6, 5a24–27). Aristotle argues that the ontology of number and time is so that their parts cannot have a position. For example, regarding time, he says: 'None of the parts of a time endures, and how could what is not enduring have any position?' (*Categories* 6, 5a27–29) It is clear that he is talking about the category of position, and by 'a position', he means something like 'a particular arrangement of the internal parts of a totality in relation to each other'. Such a position obtains when every part of that totality is situated somewhere in space (and therefore has a place). The parts of line and plane – taken as properties of physical entities – have a position in this sense. But the parts of number and time (i.e., individual numbers and moments of time) are not situated in space. They do not have a position obtained by their relational situations in space. Nevertheless, they can be distinguished by the *order* they have. The parts of time 'have a certain *order* in that one part of a time is before and another after. Similarly with a number also, in that one is counted before two and two before three; in this way, they may have a certain order, but you would certainly not find position' (*Categories* 6, 5a29–33). Thus, what Aristotle means by 'order' seems to be simply a beforeness-afterness relation by which the parts of the ordered thing can be distinguished from each other. In sum, according to Aristotle, some quantities have position and others order. He does not claim that the two types are mutually exclusive. It seems that the order between the members of a quantity might or might not be dependent (at least to some extent) on their position (if any). For example, if time has an order, a line in space is (or, at least, can be) ordered as well. Since they are topologically similar, it suffices to determine a direction for that line to attribute an order to the points of it. For example, if we assume that a line AB is extending from A to B, then for every couple of points C and D on it, C is before D if and only if AC is shorter than AD. Thus, a line in space can be considered having both position and order. Other quantities, for example an interval of time or a multitude of numbers, have order but not position. A fortiori, the order of such quantities does not depend on a position.

Given this construal of Aristotle's view, some orders are positional, others not. But if a quantity has a positional order in the sense above, it has already satisfied **WC**. This is because such an order supervenes on the mutual or relational arrangement of the parts of that quantity in space. If the parts of a quantity fail to exist altogether, a fortiori, they fail to exist altogether in space. Therefore, talking about their mutual arrangement in space does not make sense. They do not have a position, nor do they have, hence, a positional order.

Al-Fārābī (d. 950), in his *Bezels of Wisdom* (1985, p. 61, ll. 6–y), contends that the existence of infinities in 'created things which has a place (*makāna*) and an order (*rutbata*)' is impossible.[50] If a quantity has a positional order in the Aristotelian sense delineated above, it satisfies both of the conditions proposed by al-Fārābī and must be finite. However, it must be noted that he does not propose these conditions in connection to the Mapping Argument. To my knowledge, he has never discussed this particular argument in any of his works. So, it is unclear what his justification is for the claim that having position and order implies finitude.

Ibn Sīnā has scrutinised the notions of ORDER and POSITION in connection to quantities in *The Categories* of The Healing (1959, chapter IV.1, pp. 127–30). He explicitly links these notions to the Mapping Argument by claiming (in several places, though with different wordings) that this argument does not apply to quantities that are not ordered either in nature (*fī al-ṭab'*) or in position (*fī al-waḍ'*). The contrast between 'order in nature' and 'order in position' in this context can be spelt out in at least two different ways. According to one interpretation, if something has a positional order, in the sense that it has an order imposed by the position of its parts, it has an order in position. By contrast, if something has a natural order, in the sense that it has an order imposed by the

[50] Kohler (2006, p. 97) claims that from the references to one of al-Fārābī's lost treatises, that is, *On Changing Beings*, by Ibn Rushd and Maimonides, it appears that al-Fārābī 'has set two conditions for the impossibility of an infinite series or an actual infinite number: the members of this series must be ordered and they must exist simultaneously'. But it seems to me that what Ibn Rushd and Maimonides have said about al-Fārābī's view is not exactly what Kohler says.

nature or essence of its parts, it has an order in nature. This interpretation better fits the historical background narrated above. Nevertheless, it overlooks the possibility of having quantities that are neither positionally nor naturally ordered but still can be conventionally ordered. If the Arabic term '*waḍ*'' (i.e., position) is understood in the more general sense of convention and supposition instead of the restricted sense of the category of position, the contrast between 'order in nature' and 'order in position' can be interpreted as the contrast between a natural order and a conventional order. For two reasons, the latter interpretation is preferable to the former. First, instead of '*waḍ*'', Ibn Sīnā has sometimes used '*farḍ*', which less equivocally means supposition and has no relevance to the category of position.[51] Second, as we will shortly see, the applicability of the mapping technique to a quantity depends on whether or not it can be ordered; it does not matter whether this order is natural, positional (in the categorical sense), or conventional.

It is crucial to point out that having an order seems to be necessary only for the applicability of the multitude version of the Mapping Argument. It does not seem to play any significant role in the magnitude version of this argument. In the multitude version, to compare two multitudes A and B (or, more precisely, multitude A and its proper submultitudes B), we need to put them in a one-to-one correspondence by pairing each member of A with one and only one member of B. To achieve this goal, there must be procedures by which we can select the members of these multitudes one after another for pairing with each other: the first member of A with the first member of B, the second member of A with the second member of B, and so on. The mere possibility of mapping one multitude upon another in this way establishes the possibility of their being ordered. If the members of a multitude cannot be ordered, they cannot be paired with the members of another multitude one by one. Accordingly, the mapping technique cannot be employed to compare such a multitude with another to see whether or not they are equal. This means that we can appeal to **CN4** to establish the equality of two multitudes only if they can be ordered.

Quite differently, to examine the equality of two magnitudes by employing the mapping technique, we only need to superpose one of them upon another and check if any part of any of them remains uncovered by the other. Having an order does not seem to play any crucial role in mapping a magnitude upon another. We can, for example, examine the equality of two triangular planes in this way without considering any specific order for the points on these planes (Fig. 7).

[51] See Zarepour (forthcoming, section IV).

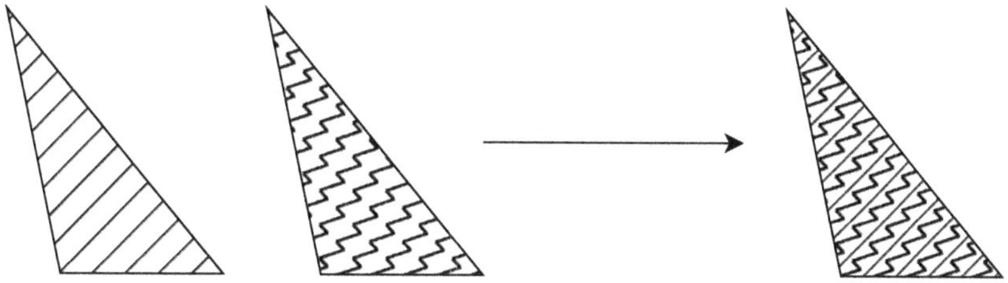

Figure 7 The two triangles are equal because when one is mapped upon another, no part of one remains uncovered by the other.

Putting all of the above observations together, it seems that, according to Ibn Sīnā, the Mapping Argument cannot establish the impossibility of an infinite multitude S unless it satisfies not only **WC** but also what is called 'the ordering condition'. A quantity S satisfies this condition if the following description is true of it:

Ordering Condition (OC): The members of S are (or, at least, can be) ordered.

Thus, according to Ibn Sīnā, any infinite magnitude that satisfies **WC** and any infinite multitude that satisfies both **WC** and **OC** are impossible.[52] As an example of a multitude whose infinitude cannot be rejected by the Mapping Argument because it does not satisfy **OC**, Ibn Sīnā has mentioned the multitude of angels and devils. He has explicitly conceded, in *The Salvation* (1985, chapter IV.2, p. 246, ll. 5–7), that the multitude of angels and devils 'is susceptible to increase, but this susceptibility does not make the [the application of] the mapping [technique] permissible; for what has no order in either nature or position is not susceptible to [the use] of the mapping [technique]'. Apparently, Ibn Sīnā believes that although the multitude of angels and devils satisfy **WC**, it fails to satisfy **OC**. Therefore, we cannot deny the possibility of its infinitude by appealing to the Mapping Argument. It is worth noting that Ibn Sīnā does not simply say that the mapping argument cannot reject the infinitude of the multitude of angels and devils because the members of this multitude are immaterial and, therefore, do not have a position (in its categorical sense). One might interpret this as a sign that, unlike some later medieval thinkers, Ibn Sīnā does not take materiality or having a position as one of the applicability conditions of the Mapping Argument. A quantity S satisfies what I call 'the materiality condition' if the following description is true of it:

[52] For more details on why Ibn Sīnā must be interpreted as considering **OC** as a condition for the applicability of only the multitude version of the Mapping Argument, despite that he has never explicitly presented this version of the Mapping Argument, see Zarepour (2020, forthcoming).

Materiality Condition (MTC): All the parts of S exist in the material world.

Ibn Sīnā does not explicitly mention **MTC** as a necessary condition for the applicability of the Mapping Argument. However, the assumption that Ibn Sīnā does not take **MTC** to be necessary for the applicability of the Mapping Argument jeopardises the overall consistency of his philosophy. If **MTC** is not necessary for the applicability of the Mapping Argument, then it must be accepted that no multitude of immaterial entities that satisfy **WC** and **OC** can be infinite. This means that there can be no multitude of souls that are ordered and coexist together. Now, if one can show that other elements of Ibn Sīnā's philosophy imply the possibility of the existence of such a multitude, then it will be established that his philosophy suffers from internal inconsistency. We will soon see that al-Ghazālī has actually established that Ibn Sīnā's philosophy implies the possibility of the existence of an infinite multitude of souls that satisfies both **WC** and **OC**. That is why I have elsewhere (Zarepour 2020, section 4.3) suggested that to preserve the internal consistency of Ibn Sīnā's philosophy, we have to interpret him as endorsing **MTC**.

The Mapping Argument and its applicability conditions were the subjects of stimulating debates in various traditions of medieval philosophy.[53] Ibn Sīnā's pupil, Bahmanyār Ibn al-Marzubān (d. 1066), in *The Attainment* (1996, pp. 557–58), proposes the same applicability conditions for the Mapping Argument as his teacher. Al-Ghazālī was also well familiar with the Mapping Argument. He has presented a version of this argument in *The Aims of the Philosophers* (2000a, pp. 97–98). And, it was probably through the translation of this book in the third quarter of the twelfth century that the core idea of this argument was transmitted to the Latin tradition.[54] In the Fourth Discussion of *The Incoherence of the Philosophers*, al-Ghazālī refers to the issue of the orderability of the multitude of human souls. He thinks that if the world has no temporal beginning, then it is, in principle, possible to have an infinite multitude of human souls that satisfies both **WC** and **OC**. The multitude he introduces can have a conventional order, which is not due to either the nature of human souls or their position.

T17. Al-Ghazālī (2000b, *The Incoherence of the Philosophers*, p. 81)

> The past days and nights are infinite [if the world has no temporal beginning]. Thus, if we suppose the [coming into] existence of a single soul in each day and night, what has come into existence up to the present would be infinite, being realised in an order of existence that is one [coming into existence] after another.

[53] For the evolution of Ibn Sīnā's own views regarding this argument throughout his career, see Zarepour (forthcoming).

[54] This claim has extensively been discussed by Mancosu (forthcoming).

Suppose the world has no temporal beginning, and every day and night, one and only one soul comes into existence. This implies that the multitude of human souls who have come into existence so far is infinite. Moreover, all the members of this multitude coexist together at present. This is because, according to Ibn Sīnā, who is the target of al-Ghazālī's criticism, souls never perish. After coming into existence, a human soul will continue to exist forever, even when the body associated with that soul dies and perishes. This indicates that the multitude in question satisfies **WC**. Finally, by appealing to the natural order of days and nights, we can put a conventional order on the members of the multitude in question. This means that **OC** can be satisfied as well. In this imaginary scenario, we have an infinite multitude of souls that satisfy both **WC** and **OC**. But this contradicts the Mapping Argument. Accordingly, if we insist not to reject the soundness of this argument, we have to reject either the eternity of the world or the immortality of the soul. In any case, at least one of the doctrines endorsed by Ibn Sīnā must be rejected. As it is well known, al-Ghazālī himself denies the eternity of the world but endorses the soul's immortality.[55] However, it must be recalled that Al-Ghazālī's line of reasoning is compelling only if **MTC** is not taken (by Ibn Sīnā) to be needed for the soundness of the Mapping Argument. If, for example, the mereology of the immaterial entities is so different from the material ones that whole-part equality (when equality is understood in the sense of correspondence as mentioned in **CN4**) is not necessarily absurd in the immaterial realm, then the infinitude of the multitude of immaterial entities like souls cannot be rejected by the Mapping Argument, regardless of whether or not the multitude in question satisfies **WC** and **OC**.

Al-Shahrastānī has presented the Mapping Argument in several works. In his *Book of Religious and Philosophical Sects* (1846, vol. 2, p. 403; see in particular ll. 9 and 19–20), he discusses Ibn Sīnā's account of the Mapping Argument and explicitly mentions that, according to Ibn Sīnā, the ordering condition is necessary for the applicability of the mapping technique. Moreover, he points out that the faculty of estimation is in charge of carrying out the mapping process in the case of infinite quantities. That is exactly why he thinks having a position – in its categorical sense – or, equivalently, the fulfilment of **MTC** is not necessary for the applicability of the Mapping Argument. Al-Shahrastānī contends, in his *Struggling with the Philosophers* (2001, p. 109), that when we argue against the infinitude of a body (which, being a body, necessarily has a position) by the

[55] Al-Ghazālī, in his *Moderation in Belief* (2013, pp. 27–40), presents an argument for the existence of God, one of whose premises is that the world has come into existence at a certain time and has a temporal beginning. A reconstruction of this argument, which is now known as the *Kalām Cosmological Argument*, is proposed by Craig (1979). On al-Ghazālī's view regarding the infinite number of souls, see Marmura (1960) and Zarepour (2020, section 4).

Mapping Argument, we apply the mapping technique to an imaginary line existing in the body we have hypothesised. However, 'what you suppose regarding an imaginary line is possible to be supposed regarding an imaginary number [i.e., multitude]'. And, this is valid regardless of whether or not the members of the multitude in question have a position. T15 is immediately mentioned after this line of argument to support the claim that **MTC** is not necessary for the Mapping Argument. Although al-Shahrastānī does not explicitly mention this, the same line of reasoning demonstrates that even **EEC** and **WC** are not necessary for the applicability of the Mapping Argument. By our imagination, we can apply the Mapping Argument to infinities that are supposed to exist only in our mind and to the cross-temporal mereological sum of things that do not coexist. That is why al-Shahrastānī (2001, *Struggling with the Philosophers*, p. 107–08) thinks the Mapping Argument applies to time and refutes the eternity of the world. By contrast with Ibn Sīnā, al-Shahrastānī believes that this argument establishes the finitude of the chain of the causal ancestors of an existent, regardless of whether the causes in question are efficient or material. For Ibn Sīnā, in contrast to material causation, which is a diachronic relation, efficient causation is a synchronic relation (Zarepour 2022b, section 3.4). Accordingly, although everything exists simultaneously with its efficient cause, the material cause of that thing is temporally prior to it. This means that the chain of the causal ancestors of an existent fulfils **WC** only if the causes in the chain are efficient rather than material. Thus, Ibn Sīnā thinks that the Mapping Argument establishes the finitude of the chain of efficient causes but not the chain of material causes.[56] Rejecting the necessity of **WC** for the applicability of the Mapping Argument, al-Shahrastānī (2001, *Struggling with the Philosophers*, p. 107–08) insists that the Mapping Argument equally applies to both of those chains and establishes that neither can be infinite. Moreover, he seems inclined to accept that every quantity can be ordered and, therefore, **OC** is not necessary for the applicability of the Mapping Argument (Lammer 2018, section 3).

Abu-l-Barakāt al-Baghdādī (d. 1165), an eminent Jewish philosopher who converted to Islam later in his life, has mentioned the Mapping Argument in his famous *The Considered*. But he thinks that this argument does not work:

[56] This position was later upheld by Thomas Aquinas. He believes motion and time can, in principle, be infinite because they fail to satisfy **WC**. Therefore, if time is indeed infinite, there can, again in principle, be a series of things that are casually connected to each other in a diachronic sense of causation. See Aquinas (2006, *Summa Theologiae*, Ia. 7, 3, p. 105 and 4, p. 107) and Cohoe (2013). Note that although Aquinas believes that time *can be* infinite, he does not believe it *is* infinite. He thinks that the *possibility* of the infinity of time can be defended philosophically. Nevertheless, the infinity of time – or, equivalently, the world's eternity – can neither be established nor rejected by philosophical arguments. On the subtleties of Aquinas's view regarding the eternity of the world, see İskenderoğlu (2002, chapter 3) and McGinnis (2014).

T18. Al-Baghdādī (1938, *The Considered*, vol. 2, p. 85)

> It is a fallacious argument because it is completed by moving the line and dragging it inasmuch as it falls short until it coincides with the initial end. However, motion is not conceivable for infinity. If a motion is conceived for it, its end will move along with the totality of it. If it rests with the extension [it has] and does not move in the opposite direction, the statement [of the argument] is useless. If [on the other hand] it is dragged from the opposite end and moves, then it has an end and its [i.e., that end's] place will be vacated so that it [i.e., the moving line] falls short of the other [line]. But there is no end or movement in length for it. The estimation cannot imagine the motion of the cut end to correspond to the uncut end unless it imagines it as a finite [line] so that the other limit moves, being dragged together with the initial limit. Otherwise, it rests superseded [from the other line] while it is in its position motionless. So, the argument is not established.

Suppose we employ the mapping technique to show that the infinite line AB, which starts from A and extends infinitely in the direction of B, is equal to its proper part CB, which begins from C and extends infinitely in the direction of B. To complete the mapping process, we must move line CB so that C coincides with A. Al-Baghdādī believes that since CB is infinite, such a movement is impossible. Therefore, the mapping process cannot be completed, and the argument fails. He argues that CB does not move unless all parts of it move together. This means that the motion must happen not only for C but also in the direction of B. However, he thinks that no motion can happen in the direction of B unless we assume B as a limit. But this means that CB has two limits and is finite. We cannot even imagine CB in motion unless we conceive it as a finite line. Al-Baghdādī's reasoning here does not make much sense from our modern perspective. Nevertheless, his discussion introduced another condition that he and many other medieval thinkers found necessary for the applicability of the Mapping Argument. A quantity S satisfies this condition – which I call 'the movability condition' – if the following description is true of it:

Movability Condition (MVC): All the parts of S are movable simultaneously.

Al-Baghdādī believes that to map CB upon AB we need to move all the parts of CB together. However, this cannot happen, even in our imagination, unless we assume that CB is finite. Thus, if CB is infinite, it does not satisfy **MVC**, or so he suggests. As a result, from the outset, the mapping technique is not applicable to infinite quantities.[57]

[57] Apparently, al-Baghdādī thinks that **MVC** is necessary not only for the magnitude version of the Mapping Argument but also for its multitude version. It is worth noting that some later Muslim thinkers appealed to **MVC** to provide solutions for challenging theological problems. For example, some philosophers and theologians try to show that although the Mapping Argument

Shihāb al-Dīn al-Suhrawardī (d. 1191) presents another version of the Mapping Argument in his *The Philosophy of Illumination* (1999, section I.3, p. 44), which goes as follows: consider a series of objects that satisfies both **WC** and **OC**. Remove a finite number of these objects from somewhere in the middle of the series and connect the remaining parts to each other (or, more precisely, consider the two remaining subseries in continuity with each other as a new ordered series). Now, employing the mapping technique, compare the size of the new series with the initial series. If the new series is equal to the initial one, then **CN5** is violated. Thus, the new series must fall short of the initial one. However, since the new series is obtained by removing only a finite part of the initial series, this indicates that the initial series must also be finite. Thus, the existence of an infinite series is impossible.

As I stated earlier, al-Rāzī has discussed and defended the Mapping Argument in many places in his oeuvre. For example, al-Rāzī presents this argument in *Eastern Investigation* (1990, vol. 1, pp. 306–07) and *Commentary on* Fountains of Wisdom (1994, vol. 2, pp. 49–50). Most of the objections against these arguments raised and evaluated in these two books are similar. He contends that **MVC** is not necessary for the applicability of this argument because the process of comparison through the mapping technique can be made entirely in the mind and by merely appealing to the intellectual ranks (*al-marātib al-ʿaqliyya*) that can be assigned to the parts of the infinities one of which is supposed to be mapped upon the other.[58] By contrast, he thinks that **OC** is necessary for the applicability of the Mapping Argument. His best defence of this view can be found in a discussion of the applicability of the Mapping Argument to the multitude of human souls.[59] As I mentioned earlier, philosophers like Ibn Sīnā believe that human souls have temporal origination, but they never perish after coming into existence. This implies that the multitude of human souls who existed one hundred years ago (call it M_{-100}) is smaller than the multitude of souls who exist now (call it M_0). Now, one might think that by applying the mapping technique, we can establish the finitude of M_0 (and, consequently, M_{-100}). Al-Rāzī reports that the sages (*al-ḥukamā*) do not accept this because these multitudes have no order either in nature or in position. He then states

establishes things like the finitude of the past, it fails to establish the finitude of the multitude of the objects of God's knowledge and/or power. This is because the objects of God's knowledge and/or power do not satisfy **MVC**, or so those scholars suggest. See, for example, Beşikci (forthcoming).

[58] This objection – which argues that the Mapping Argument is unsound because (a) satisfying **MVC** is essential for the mapping technique to be applicable and (b) infinite entities do not meet **MVC** – is raised and responded to, among other places, in al-Rāzī (1994, *Commentary on* Fountains of Wisdom, vol. 2, pp. 50 and 53–54).

[59] This discussion is included in the second objection to the mapping argument that al-Rāzī anticipates and blocks. See al-Rāzī (1994, *Commentary on* Fountains of Wisdom, vol. 2, pp. 50–51 and 54–56).

that some theologians find this manoeuvre extremely weak because they think that regardless of whether or not these multitudes are ordered, M_{-100} is smaller than M_0, and this suffices to prove that M_{-100} is finite. Coupling this with the fact that since a hundred years ago only a finite number of souls have come into existence, we can conclude that M_0 is finite too. However, al-Rāzī himself does not find such an approach plausible. He says that 'the criteria mentioned by the sages is indeed valid'. Consider the following syllogism:

(8) Everything that falls short of another thing is finite.
(9) A falls short of B.

Therefore:

(10) A is finite.

Al-Rāzī focuses on the meaning of 'finitude' in this syllogism and says:

> T19. Al-Rāzī (1994, *Commentary on* Fountains of Wisdom, vol. 2, pp. 55–56)
>
> If we mean by its being finite that something is realised in others that is not realised in it, then the meaning of it being finite is that it falls short of others. Then, in this syllogism, the major [term] would be the same as the middle [term]. And, if what we mean by that is the necessity of what falls short ending up at a rank beyond which nothing else is left, [then] this can be thought of [only] in what has an order in position or in nature. This meaning is not realised in what is not like this [i.e., in non-ordered things]. If we intend a third meaning, it would not be intelligible.

If we take the meaning of 'finitude' to be 'falling short of another thing', then (8) would be a self-evident (indeed, tautologously true) proposition. However, al-Rāzī seems to think that (8) is not a self-evident proposition and must be demonstrated. Apparently, he thinks that to draw the finitude of A from that A falls short of B, A must have a part that corresponds to part of B that has a finite rank.[60] And he thinks that this cannot happen unless A and B are ordered. So, he thinks that **OC** is a necessary condition for the applicability of the Mapping Argument. He also thinks that **WC** is necessary for the applicability of this argument. That is why he thinks this argument cannot establish the impossibility of the multitude of past events. They fail to exist simultaneously. Thus, their infinitude is compatible with the soundness of the Mapping Argument, whose aim, according to al-Rāzī, is to establish the impossibility of infinities that satisfy **WC**, among other conditions.[61]

[60] It is worth highlighting that he does not try to demonstrate (8) based on **EI**, even though it seems that the former claim is a straightforward consequence of the latter.

[61] See his discussion of the third and seventh possible objections to the Mapping Argument in (1994, *Commentary on* Fountains of Wisdom, vol. 2, pp. 51–52 and 56–57). It must be noted, however, that al-Rāzī does not take the inapplicability of this argument to the past events (or, more generally,

It is worth mentioning that al-Rāzī does not think that the mapping technique applies to *every* ordered infinity, even if all its parts coexist. In particular, he does not think that the Mapping Argument can establish the finitude of the multitude of all natural numbers. In response to the objection described in T16, al-Rāzī (1994, *Commentary on* Fountains of Wisdom, vol. 2, pp. 57) says that the Mapping Argument does not apply to numbers because they do not exist in the extramental world. So, it seems that he considers **EEC** necessary for the applicability of numbers. Apparently, he thinks that numbers are mind-dependent existents. Therefore, failing to satisfy **EEC**, the multitude of all numbers can, in principle, be actually infinite. However, as a matter of fact, this multitude does not form an actual infinity even in our minds. Al-Rāzī (1994, *Commentary on* Fountains of Wisdom, vol. 2, p. 54) argues that the multitude of all numbers – as a whole – neither exists in the extramental realm nor even in the mind. He explicitly mentions that the mind is unable to present an infinite number of things all together at the same time.[62] Put differently, he thinks that the multitude of natural numbers do not satisfy **WC** either in the extramental world or even in our mind.

It seems that according to al-Rāzī, all numbers can coexist in an infinite mind like God's.[63] This does not jeopardise the soundness of the Mapping Argument because it does not apply to any multitude that fails to satisfy **EEC**. This implies that infinite sets of mind-dependent objects are not impossible. Given that al-Rāzī considers mathematical objects to be mind-dependent, he does not seem to have any problem with infinitism in mathematics. Endorsing a radically different ontology of mathematics, Ibn Sīnā seems to be a finitist about mathematics. He believes that mathematical objects are properties of physical objects. Since there cannot be any infinite body, there cannot be any infinite magnitude. In particular, there cannot be any infinite geometrical line. Geometrical entities do not exist independently from physical objects. Similarly, since (a) the multitude of all physical objects in the world is finite and (b) numbers are properties of the

to time) as a justification for the eternity of the world. Al-Rāzī neither straightforwardly accepts nor rejects the eternity of the world. To a large extent similar to Aquinas, he believes that both the philosophical arguments for the eternity of the world and those for its temporal origination have significant shortcomings, making them indecisive. Moreover, al-Rāzī argues that neither doctrine is necessary for religious (and, in particular, Islamic) belief. For al-Rāzī's views on the eternity of the world and their philosophical affinities with Aquinas's position, see İskenderoğlu (2002). Refraining from a straightforward endorsement of either the eternity of the world or its temporal origination was not a rare approach in medieval philosophy. Abu-l-Barakāt al-Baghdādī and Maimonides are other well-known representatives of this approach.

62 See also al-Rāzī (1990, *Eastern Investigation*, vol. 1, p. 311).

63 I do not know if he has ever explicitly affirmed the existence of the infinite multitude of numbers in God's mind. Nevertheless, even if al-Rāzī denies this, it would not be because he thinks God cannot grasp and entertain an infinite number of mental objects altogether. He believes that the number of the objects of God's knowledge is infinite. See, for example, al-Rāzī (1990, *Eastern Investigation*, vol. 1, p. 310).

multitudes of objects, the multitude of all numbers existing in the world is finite. However, this multitude is potentially infinite because the number of existing physical objects can, in principle, increase with new objects coming into existence. Accordingly, the multitude of all numbers existing in the world can, in principle, become bigger boundlessly. Nevertheless, this multitude is never actually infinite. It might be possible (if the mind's capacity allows) to imagine a number greater than the number of all the physical objects existing in the world or a geometrical shape bigger than the world. Nevertheless, such imaginations do not bring those mathematical objects into existence. Ibn Sīnā is a finitist, not only about physics but also about mathematics.[64]

Returning to al-Rāzī's discussion of the Mapping Argument, a couple of other objections to this argument that he anticipates and rebuts are worth mentioning. For example, in the fifth objection to this argument in his *Commentary on* Fountains of Wisdom, al-Rāzī says:

T20. al-Rāzī, *Commentary on* Fountains of Wisdom (1994, vol. 2, p. 51)

> [The number resulting from] doubling a thousand repeatedly and infinitely is less than [the number resulting from] doubling two thousand repeatedly and infinitely. And whatever is less than something other than itself is finite. So, an infinite is finite. This is absurd.[65]

The relevance of this objection to the Mapping Argument is not quite clear. However, one possible explanation goes as follows: assume that *m* and *n* are two infinite numbers that are made by doubling, respectively, a thousand and two thousand repeatedly and infinitely. Moreover, assume that M and N are the multitudes of all numbers from 1 to, respectively, *m* and *n*. M and N are two ordered multitudes whose sizes can be compared by the mapping technique. The objector insists that *m* is smaller than *n*. Accordingly, M is a proper submultitude of N. Thus, if we compare the two multitudes by the mapping technique, M falls short of N, and some of the numbers in N remain unpaired. This means that M and, consequently, *m* must be finite. But this is absurd because the number resulting from doubling one thousand repeatedly and infinitely is not finite. To show that this objection is untenable al-Rāzī says:

T21. Al-Rāzī (1994, *Commentary on* Fountains of Wisdom, vol. 2, pp. 56–57)

> These numbers do not exist in the extramental world or even in the mind. They are present in the intellect by relating the meaning of infinity to the meaning of doubling. And this is nothing other than relating a meaning to a meaning. This is contrary to the bodies and causes. They exist in the extramental world.

[64] On this interpretation of Ibn Sīnā's ontology of mathematics, see Zarepour (2016).
[65] This objection is also mentioned in al-Rāzī (1990, *Eastern Investigation*, vol. 1, p. 310).

The first two sentences of this passage seem to imply that a description like 'the number resulting from doubling a thousand repeatedly and infinitely' is an empty description. It is made by putting the notions of DOUBLING and INFINITY together, but it does not refer to anything existing either in the extramental world or even in the mind. In particular, it does not refer to any number. According to this reading, the objection fails apparently because it talks about infinite numbers, while it does not make sense to treat infinity as a number. Put differently, the objection fails because it relies on the assumption of the existence of infinite numbers. However, in the last two sentences of the passage, the emphasis of the response shifts from the implausibility of the latter assumption to the fact that the infinities in question fail to satisfy **EEC**. I take these sentences as stating that even if it is legitimate to take the infinities resulting from doubling a thousand and two thousand repeatedly and infinitely as infinite numbers associated with infinite multitudes, those numbers and multitudes do not exist in the extramental world. These infinite things, as mathematical objects, would be merely mental existents. In particular, the infinite multitudes in question do not satisfy **EEC**. Thus, the Mapping Argument does not apply to them.

Another objection, whose relevance to the Mapping Argument is again not straightforwardly clear, goes as follows:

> T22. al-Rāzī, *Commentary on* Fountains of Wisdom (1994, vol. 2, p. 53)
>
> One is a half of two, a third of three, a fourth of four, and so on *ad infinitum* (*ilā mā lā nihāyah lah*) in terms of ratios. Thus, we say: there is no doubt that the sum of these ratios with the deduction of the first ten of them is less than this sum without that deduction. This makes the sum of these ratios finite, though we clarified that they are infinite. This is absurd.

It seems that the rational numbers and the sums involved in this scenario are assumed to be represented by magnitudes or multitudes. Indeed, it is hard to see how this objection could be relevant to the mapping argument without this assumption. The passage can be interpreted in two different ways, making two different mathematical points. According to the first interpretation, the ratios the objector mentions in the first sentence of the passage are 1/2, 1/3, 1/4, and so on, and the sums that are compared are the following ones:

$$S_2 = 1/2 + 1/3 + 1/4 + \dots$$

$$S_{12} = 1/12 + 1/13 + 1/14 + \dots$$

It is mathematically provable that none of the above sums converge to a finite number. Both of them are infinite. On the other hand, S_{12} is the result of the deduction of the first ten ratios of S_2 from it. Thus, $S_2 > S_{12}$. Now, if we represent S_2 and S_{12} by two magnitudes, one shorter than the other, we can apply the Mapping Argument to them and conclude that those magnitudes must be finite. But this is unacceptable. Therefore, the Mapping Argument is unsound, or so the objector might conclude.

However, I am not sure if the mathematical fact that the above series are divergent was known to al-Rāzī.[66] Thus, an interpretation of T22 that does not appeal to the divergence of S_2 and S_{12} might be preferable. According to such an interpretation, the ratios the objector talks about in the first sentence of T22 are 2/2, 3/3, 4/4, and so on, and the compared sums are the following ones:

$$S_2 = 2/2 + 3/3 + 4/4 + \ldots = 1 + 1 + 1 + \ldots.$$

$$S_{12} = 12/12 + 13/13 + 14/14 + \ldots = 1 + 1 + 1 + \ldots.$$

Both sums are infinite because they are made of an infinite number of successive additions of 1. However, the number of 1s in S_{12} is less than in S_2. Accordingly, $S_2 > S_{12}$.[67] Now, if we represent these sums by two magnitudes and compare them by the mapping technique, we must conclude that the shorter magnitude, which is represented by S_{12}, must be finite. But this conclusion is absurd. In this interpretation, S_2 and S_{12} can also be taken as the number of the elements of two infinite multitudes, one of which is a submultiple of the other. For example, S_2 and S_{12} can be taken as the number of the members of the multitudes of all natural numbers greater than 1 and 11, respectively. By applying the mapping technique to these multitudes, we can conclude that the multitude associated with S_{12} must be infinite. But this is absurd.

To block this objection, al-Rāzī (1994, *Commentary on* Fountains of Wisdom, vol. 2, p. 57) again highlights the role of **EEC** and insists that the argument developed in T22 is flawed because the rational numbers mentioned in this argument do not exist in the extramental world. This implies that the magnitudes and multitudes associated with S_2 and S_{12} do not satisfy EEC. Accordingly, their finitude cannot be established by the Mapping Argument. To summarise al-Rāzī's view regarding the Mapping Argument, he finds it plausible and considers OC, WC, and EEC necessary for its application.

---

[66] Nicole Oresme (d. 1382) is usually introduced as the first person to prove the divergence of the harmonic series (i.e., $S_1 = 1 + 1/2 + 1/3 + 1/4 + \ldots$). If this is true, then al-Rāzī could not be aware of the divergence of S_2 and S_{12}. For Oresme's proof of the divergence of the harmonic series, which was originally presented in his *Questions on the Geometry of Euclid*, see Grant (1974, p. 135).

[67] I am thankful to a reviewer who suggested this reading of the passage.

The Mapping Argument was widely discussed by many scholars in the later Islamic philosophy and theology. Many medieval Muslim theologians (particularly from the Sunni tradition) who addressed this argument believed that it could establish the impossibility of any infinity that satisfies **EEC** regardless of whether or not **MTC** and **WC** are satisfied.[68] Things with **OC** are a bit more complicated. **OC** is usually considered to be necessary for the application of the mapping technique to multitudes. It was widely accepted that the members of two multitudes could be paired one by one only if their members could be ordered. Nevertheless, like al-Shahrastānī, many Muslim theologians believed that any multitude could be ordered. Put differently, although they took **OC** as a necessary condition for the applicability of the Mapping Argument to multitudes, they believed this condition would be trivial because every multitude satisfies it. On the other hand, **OC** was usually not considered necessary for the applicability of the Mapping Argument to magnitudes. Accordingly, most post-Avicennian Muslim theologians believed that this argument rejects the infinitude of any magnitude or multitude whose parts exist in the extramental world, whether these parts coexist simultaneously or exist at different times. As a result, these scholars believed that the Mapping Argument establishes the finitude of the size and age of the world, the multitude of all human souls, and any chain of causally connected entities (in any sense of causation). Nevertheless, since many such theologians take mathematical objects to be merely mental or estimative (*wahmī*) objects, they do not take the Mapping Argument as jeopardising mathematical infinitism.[69]

To provide more specific examples, we can consider a discussion of the Mapping Argument by Jalāl al-Dīn al-Dawānī (d. 1502) in his *A Treatise on the Proof of the Necessary* (2013, pp. 139–56). He explicitly mentions that although this argument applies to the multitudes of events and human souls, it does not apply to the multitude of all numbers because they do not have extramental existence (al-Dawānī, 2013, *A Treatise on the Proof of the Necessary*, pp. 140–41). Moreover, he denies the necessity of **OC** by the following line of argument:

T23. al-Dawānī, *A Treatise on the Proof of the Necessary* (2013, p. 144).

Either [the applicability of] the mapping [technique] depends on considering individuals as [totally] differentiated [from each other] (*mufaṣṣalan*) or it is sufficient to consider them [just] as a whole (*mujmalan*). In the first case, the mapping is impossible also for the ordered. In the second case, it applies also to the non-ordered.

---

68 See Beşikci (2022, pp. 127–28).

69 On the view of Muslim theologians regarding the ontology of mathematics, see Zarepour (2022a, section 1.2).

To establish that **OC** is unnecessary, al-Dawānī puts forward a dilemma. When we are applying the mapping technique to an infinite multitude, one of the following things must be the case: either (a) it is required that we consider all the members of that multitude one by one and individually, or (b) it is not. If (a), then the mapping process can never be completed regardless of whether or not the multitude in question is ordered. This is because our finite mind cannot entertain an infinite number of things one by one and individually. On the other hand, if we can apply the mapping technique to an infinite multitude just by thinking of it as a coarse whole without considering its members one by one and individually, this means that it does not matter whether the multitude in question is ordered or not. Therefore, the mapping technique can apply even to non-ordered multitudes, or so al-Dawānī concludes. However, it seems that his reasoning is flawed. What can be concluded from the fact that we can apply the mapping technique to a multitude without considering all its members individually is, at best, that, in the application of the mapping technique, it does not matter what the exact order of the members of the multitude in question is. Put differently, it does not matter which member of the multitude comes first and which next. This means that in the application of the mapping technique to a multitude, it does not matter what the exact order of its members is. Nevertheless, this does not imply that in such an application it does not matter whether or not the multitude in question *can be* ordered. Thus, it seems that al-Dawānī's argument fails to show that **OC** is not necessary for the applicability of the mapping technique.

A more careful – though still implausible – claim regarding whether considering the members of a multitude one by one and individually is necessary for the application of the mapping technique to an infinite multitude is made by an Ottoman scholar, Khojazāda (d. 1488). He argues that in applying this technique to a multitude, we must consider all its members totally differentiated from each other and one by one only if they do not have an order either in nature or in position (in its categorical sense). On the one hand, he thinks that **OC** is indeed necessary for the applicability of the Mapping Argument. On the other hand, we cannot impose an arbitrary order on a multitude that lacks natural and positional order without considering its members one by one and individually. As a result, since our finite mind is unable to consider an infinite number of things, we cannot impose an order to an infinity that lacks natural and positional order. That is exactly why he thinks that the mapping technique is inapplicable to the multitude of human souls. Since they do not have natural and positional order, the possibility of their infinitude cannot be rejected by the Mapping Argument.[70]

[70] See Shihadeh (2011, p. 151, section 7).

Khojazāda develops the above argument against al-Ghazālī's claim that the Mapping Argument establishes the finitude of the multitude of human souls. However, it is noteworthy that if we assume, as al-Ghazālī's hypothetical scenario in T17 suggests, that in each day and night, only a single human soul comes into existence, then the natural order of days and nights is automatically transmitted to human souls. In this sense, we can say that the multitude of human souls has an order that supervenes on the natural order of day and night. So, even by Khojazāda's criteria, the mapping technique would be applicable to the multitude of human souls.[71]

As I mentioned earlier, the Mapping Argument was transmitted into both Jewish and Christian traditions. From at least the third quarter of the twelfth century (when al-Ghazālī's *The Aims of the Philosophers* was translated into Latin) onwards, many scholars writing in Latin discussed this argument. For example, the magnitude version of the Mapping Argument is presented by Alexander Neckam (also recorded as 'Nequam', d. 1217) in his *On the Nature of Things* (1863, p. 303).[72] William of Auvergne also presents the magnitude version of the Mapping Argument in his *The Universe of Creatures*. In this argument, he compares the length of two infinite lines by dragging one of them and mapping it upon another. Recall that the idea of mapping by moving was previously discussed by scholars like al-Baghdādī and al-Rāzī. William presents the mapping argument as follows: consider two parallel infinite lines. One of them starts from point A and extends infinitely in the direction of B, while the distance between A and B is one cubit. The other line starts from C and extends infinitely in the direction of D, while B corresponds to C (Fig. 8a). In the first step of the argument, William states that the infinite line starting from B must be equal to the infinite line starting from C. Otherwise – that is if one of the two lines falls short of the other – the shorter line has an endpoint and would be finite. If the line starting from B is finite, then the line starting from A would be finite, too. However, this contradicts the initial assumption. For the same reason, the line starting from C cannot be finite. This means that the lines starting from B and C correspond to each other and, given **CN4**, are equal. But the line starting from B is a part of the line starting from A. Thus, given **CN5**, the latter

[71] One might think that the Mapping Argument cannot reject the possibility that infinitely many souls come into existence together simultaneously. However, this is not acceptable from the point of view of Muslim philosophers because each soul must be associated with a body in its origination and no body can be associated with more than one soul. But if one assumes – as the majority of Muslim scholars do – that no multitude of coexisting bodies can be infinite, then there can be no infinite multitude of souls that come into existence together simultaneously. Ibn Sīnā's example of the multitude of angels and devils does not have this shortcoming because angels and devils are not assumed to be embodied at all.

[72] A discussion of Neckam's views about infinity can be found in Davenport (1999, chapter 1).

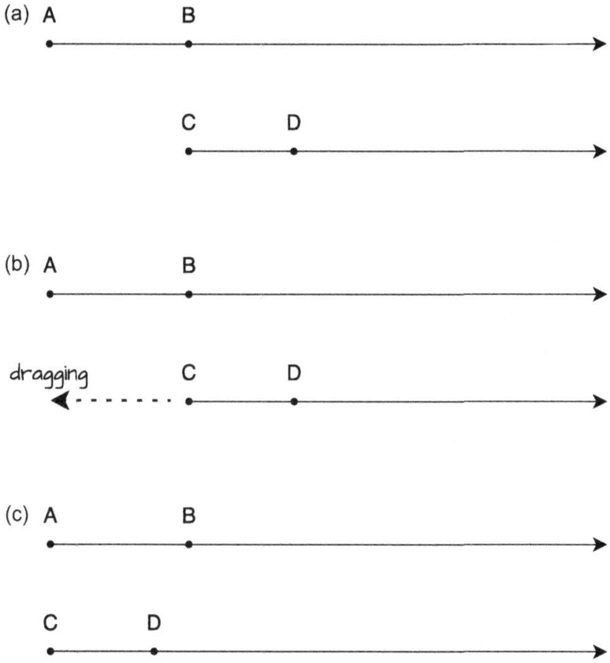

Figure 8 Mapping one line upon another by dragging and moving.

line is greater than the former. Putting these observations together, we can conclude that the line starting from A is greater than the line starting from C. In the second step of the argument, William says that by dragging the line starting from C for one cubit leftward, we can map the line starting from A upon the line starting from C (Fig. 8b). By a similar argument as what we saw in the first step, we can show that the two lines are equal to each other (Fig. 8c). But this contradicts, the result of the first step. So, the initial assumption of the existence of infinite lines must be rejected.[73]

William takes this argument to be applicable to time. This means that he does not assume that anything like **WC** is necessary for the Mapping Argument's applicability. Peter John Olivi (d. 1298) has mentioned a version of the Mapping Argument that looks like al-Kindī's version (see Murdoch 1968, 1969). Thomas Bradwardine (d. 1349), in his *De causa Dei*, has offered a version of the Mapping Argument against the eternity of the world, according to which the eternity of the world is unacceptable because if the eternity of the world implies the correspondence of the multitude of the souls of all the Popes to the multitude of all the human souls, which is absurd, or so Bradwardine thinks (Sylla 2021, section 7). Finally, to mention an example of this argument in the Jewish

[73] Mancosu (forthcoming, section 3.2) offers a detailed analysis of this argument.

tradition, we can refer to a discussion of this argument by Ḥasdai Crescas (d. 1410/11) in his *Light of the Lord* (2018, pp. 37 and 73–74). He does not find this argument plausible because he thinks that infinity is not measurable. Nor can we describe them as being greater or lesser than each other. Therefore, it seems that he does not take **CN5** to be applicable to infinities.

The cases we analysed in this section do not include all medieval engagements with the Mapping Argument. Nevertheless, they can sufficiently clarify the structure and subtleties of this argument and provide a reliable sample reflecting the general attitudes of medieval philosophers toward it. The application of the Mapping Argument to an infinite quantity S seems to have two crucial steps: (a) to compare the size of S with the size of a part of it by employing the mapping technique and establishing the equality of S to that specific part of it by appealing to **CN4**, and (b) to draw an absurdity from the whole-part equality established in the previous step by appealing to **CN5**. Interestingly, some conditions introduced for the Mapping Argument's applicability are related to the first step and the others to the second one. Specifically, **OC** and **MVC** seem to be associated with the first step. On the other hand, **WC**, **EEC**, and **MTC** seem to be related to the second step. For example, the defenders of the necessity of **OC** believe that if a multitude is not ordered, it cannot be in one-to-one correspondence with another multitude. Accordingly, we cannot compare the size of such multitudes, let alone establish their equality by appealing to **CN4**. In this sense, **OC** is entirely different from a condition like **WC**. The latter condition does not seem to have anything to do with the first step of the Mapping Argument. To show this with a specific example, consider the application of the Mapping Argument to the multitude of the past days. If the world is eternal, the multitude of all the past days until today can be put in one-to-one correspondence with the multitude of all the days before two days ago, even though these multitudes do not satisfy **WC**. So, it does not seem implausible to conclude that these two multitudes are equal in the sense of equality mentioned in **CN5**. Nevertheless, those philosophers who think that **WC** is necessary for the soundness of the Mapping Argument seem to believe that the equality of an infinity that does not satisfy **WC** with a part of itself does not have any absurd consequences.

Now, we are in a position to see how the Mapping Argument has contributed to making our conception of infinity more sophisticated. In particular, we can compare the conception of infinity hidden in the discussions of the Mapping Argument with what is presumed in the Equality Argument, on the one hand, and our modern concept of infinity, on the other. I take up this comparison in the Conclusion, to which I now turn.

5 Conclusion

Throughout this Element, we have explored two early episodes of the history of the notion of INFINITIES OF DIFFERENT SIZES by analysing various versions of two medieval arguments for finitism, which somehow employ this notion. In the Equality Argument, **EI** – namely that all infinities are equal to each other – is taken for granted. However, no effective criterion is introduced for the equality of infinities. The medieval discussions of this argument do not tell us how one can confirm that two infinities are indeed equal. It is an assumption that must be accepted with no justification. Interestingly, although no sufficient criterion for equality of infinities is introduced, a criterion for their inequality is introduced and employed. Medieval philosophers took **CN5** as implying that, like any other whole, an infinite whole is greater and, therefore, unequal to its parts, even if those parts are themselves infinite.

Taking one step forward, in the Mapping Argument, the assumption of **EI** is replaced by a sufficient criterion for the equality of infinities. The advocates of the Mapping Argument took **CN4** as implying that one infinity is equal to another if one of them can be mapped upon the other and neither exceeds the other. In the case of infinite multitudes, we saw that, in practice, this criterion was often taken as a one-to-one correspondence between the members of the two infinities in question. If two infinite multitudes can be put in a one-to-one correspondence, they are equal. Instead of claiming that all infinite multitudes are equal to each other (in terms of their size), the medieval friends of the Mapping Argument seem to be open to the idea that if we cannot put two infinite multitudes in a one-to-one correspondence, we are not justified to insist that they are equal. This does not mean that all such philosophers believed that infinities that cannot be put in a one-to-one correspondence are indeed of different sizes. Rather, they merely believed that the sizes of such infinities are not comparable to each other. From this perspective, the medieval discussions of the Mapping Argument opened up a way for considering the possibility of infinities of different sizes by introducing a criterion for the equality of infinities that, in principle, may or may not be satisfied. Nevertheless, there was still a long way to go from those ideas to our current conceptions of infinite sets of different sizes.

The next step in the history of the notion of INFINITIES OF DIFFERENT SIZES was taken by those who did not find the Mapping Argument compelling. Assume that A is an infinite submultitude of B such that they can be put in one-to-one correspondence. Now consider the following premises:

(11) Since A corresponds to B and **CN4** holds, they are equal.
(12) Since B is a part of A and **CN5** holds, A is greater than B.

From these premises, we should conclude that such infinite multitudes are impossible. However, those who did not find this argument compelling believed that the notion of BEING GREATER THAN mentioned in **CN5** and (12) is not necessarily incompatible with the notion of EQUALITY mentioned in **CN4** and (11). This motivated some medieval philosophers to argue that the notion of BEING GREATER THAN can be understood in different senses, some of which are perfectly compatible with the notion of EQUALITY in the sense of correspondence. In particular, they tried to show that there is a legitimate notion of BEING GREATER THAN that allows A to be greater than B while they still correspond to each other. The attempts to provide clear definitions of such notions should be considered the next stage of the historical evolution of the notion of INFINITIES OF DIFFERENT SIZES.[74] Having a more limited focus, I could not discuss that stage in this Element.

There are still a couple of other points that seem to be worth highlighting before closing this Element. First, the multitude version of the Mapping Argument clearly shows that medieval philosophers were aware of the characteristic feature of infinite sets that is highlighted in Dedekind's definition of infinity. As is put by Reck (2023), a 'set of objects is infinite – "Dedekind-infinite", as we now say – if it can be mapped one-to-one onto a proper subset of itself'. Medieval philosophers' notion of MULTITUDE might not completely fit the modern notion of SET. Nevertheless, it is striking that many medieval philosophers (who found the multitude version of the Mapping Argument compelling) believed that every infinite multitude can be in one-to-one correspondence with some of its proper submultitude. To my knowledge, unlike Dedekind, no medieval philosopher has mentioned this characteristic in a *definition* of infinite multitudes. Indeed, the defenders of the Mapping Argument somehow thought that this characteristic is precisely what makes the instantiation of infinite multitudes impossible. Nevertheless, the mere fact that they knew that infinite multitudes correspond with some of their submultitudes shows that medieval philosophers, compared to, for example, Ancient Greek philosophers, held a conception of infinity that more closely resembles the modern understanding of this notion.

Second, another striking fact about the medieval conception of infinity is that some medieval philosophers have taken **OC** as necessary for the applicability of the mapping technique. This means that we cannot talk about whether or not multitudes correspond to each other unless they are ordered. Borrowing the terminology of the modern set theory, they apparently believed that *ordinality* is

[74] Such attempts can be seen in the works of Latin philosophers like Henry of Harclay, William of Alnwick (d. 1333), and Gregory of Rimini (d. 1358). See Murdoch (1982, pp. 571–72).

prior to *cardinality*. Some philosophers, like Ibn Sīnā, thought that not every multitude can be ordered, while others, like al-Shahrastānī, believed that everything can be ordered.

This Element aimed to explore early medieval encounters with the notion of INFINITIES OF DIFFERENT SIZES through the lens of two medieval arguments for finitism. Admittedly, many other important and interesting things about the medieval encounters with this notion are yet to be explored in other works. Nevertheless, I hope the present study has shed some light on at least a few dark corners of the tantalising history of infinities of different sizes and encourages other scholars to explore other corners I could not explore.

Abbreviations

CN4	Common Notion 4
CN5	Common Notion 5
EI	Equality of Infinities
EEC	Extramental Existence Condition
NIM	Numericality of Infinite Multitudes
MTC	Materiality Condition
MVC	Movability Condition
OC	Ordering Condition
WC	Wholeness Condition

Ancient and Medieval Thinkers Discussed in This Element

Aristotle (d. 322 BCE)
Lucretius (d. circa 55 BCE)
Plutarch (d. circa 120)
Proclus (d. 485)
Simplicius (d. 560)
John Philoponus (d. 570)
al-Ḥajjāj Ibn Yūsuf Ibn Maṭar (d. 833)
Ibrāhīm al-Naẓẓām (d. circa 845)
al-Kindī (d. 870)
Thābit Ibn Qurra al-Ḥarrānī (d. 901)
Isḥāq Ibn Ḥunayn (d. circa 910)
al-Khayyāt (d. circa 910)
al-Fārābī (d. 950)
Yaḥyā Ibn ʿAdī (d. 974)
ʿAbd al-Qāhir al-Baghdādī (d. 1037)
Ibn Sīnā = Avicenna (d. 1037)
Bahmanyār Ibn al-Marzubān (d. 1066)
al-Ghazālī (d. 1111)
Bachya Ben Joseph Ibn Paquda = Baḥy Ibn Yūsuf Ibn Bāqūda (d. 1120)
Ibn Bājja = Avempace (d. 1138)
Adelard of Bath (d. 1152?)
Muhammad Ibn ʿAbd al-Karīm al-Shahrastānī (d. 1153)
Peter Lombard (d. 1160)
Abu-l-Barakāt al-Baghdādī (d. 1165)
Shihāb al-Dīn al-Suhrawardī (d. 1191)
Ibn Rushd = Averroes (d. 1198)
Moses Maimonides = Mūsa Ibn Maymūn (d. 1204)
Fakhr al-Dīn al-Rāzī (d. 1210)
Alexander Neckam = Alexander Nequam (d. 1217)
William of Auvergne (d. 1249)
Bonaventure (d. 1274)
Naṣīr al-Dīn al-Ṭūsī (d. 1274)
Thomas Aquinas (d. 1274)
Roger Bacon (d. 1292)

John Peckham (d. 1292)
Peter John Olivi (d. 1298)
Muḥammad al-Tabrīzī (d. 13th century)
Henry of Harclay (d. 1317)
William of Alnwick (d. 1333)
Gersonides (d. 1344)
Thomas Bradwardine (d. 1349)
Gregory of Rimini (d. 1358)
Nicole Oresme (d. 1382)
Isac ben Nathan of Cordoba (d. 14th century)
Ḥasdai Crescas (d. 1410/11)
Khojazāda (d. 1488)
Jalāl al-Dīn al-Dawānī (d. 1502)

References

Primary References

Adamson, P. (2007) *Al-Kindī*. Oxford: Oxford University Press.

Aquinas, Thomas (2006) *Summa Theologiae Ia. 2–11, Volume 2, Existence and Nature of God*. Edited and translated by T. McDermott. Cambridge: Cambridge University Press.

Aristotle (1984) *The Complete Works of Aristotle: The Revised Oxford Translation*. Edited by J. Barnes. Princeton, NJ: Princeton University Press.

Bacon, Roger (1928) *The Opus Majus of Roger Bacon*. Translated by R. B. Burke. Two Vols. Philadelphia: University of Pennsylvania Press.

Bacon, Roger (2012) *Opus Tertium*, in *Fr. Rogeri Bacon Opera Quædam Hactenus Inedita*. Edited by J. S. Brewer. Cambridge: Cambridge University Press, pp. 3–310.

al-Baghdādī, Abu-l-Barakāt (1938) *al-Muʿtabar fi-l-ḥikma* [*The Considered*]. Edited by A. al-ʿAlawī al-Ḥaḍramī, Aḥmad Ibn Muḥammad al-Yamānī, and Zayn al-ʿĀbidīn al-Musāwī. Three Vols. Hyderabad: Dāʾirat al-maʿārif al-ʿuthmāniyya.

al-Baghdādī, ʿAbd al-Qāhir (1981) *Uṣūl al-dīn* [*The Principles of Religion*]. Beirut: Dār al-kutub al-ʿilmiyya.

Bahmanyār Ibn al-Marzubān (1996) *Al-Taḥṣīl* [*The Attainment*]. Edited by M. Muṭahharī. Tehran: Tehran University Press.

Bonaventure (1882) *Commentaria in Quatuor Libros Sententiarum* [*Commentary on the Four Books of the Sentences*], in *Opera Omnia*. Edited by the Fathers of Collegium St. Bonaventure. Vol. 1. Quaracchi: ex typographia Collegii St. Bonaventurae.

Bonaventure (1964) *On the Eternity of the World (De Aeternitate Mundi)*. Translated by P. M. Byrne. Milwaukee, WI: Marquette University Press.

Crescas, Ḥasdai (2018) *Light of the Lord (Or Hashem)*. Translated by R. Weiss. Oxford: Oxford University Press.

al-Dawānī, Jalāl al-Dīn (2013) *Risāla fī ithbāt al-wājib* [*A Treatise on the Proof of the Necessary*]. Edited by M. A. Abū Ghūsh. Amman: Dār al-nūr al-mubīn lil-dirāsāt wa-l-nashr.

Euclid (1908) *The Thirteen Books of Euclid's Elements*. Translated by T. L. Heath. Cambridge: Cambridge University Press.

al-Fārābī (1985). *Fuṣūṣ al-ḥikam* [*Bezels of Wisdom*]. Edited by M. Ḥ. ĀL Yāsīn. Second Ed. Qum: Bīdār Press.

al-Ghazālī (2000a) *Maqāṣid al-falāsifa [The Aims of the Philosophers]*. Edited by M. Bījū. Damascus: Maṭba'a al-ṣabāḥ.

al-Ghazālī (2000b) *The Incoherence of the Philosophers*. Edited and translated by M. E. Marmura. Provo, UT: Brigham Young University Press.

al-Ghazālī (2013) *Moderation in Belief*. Translated with an interpretive essay and notes by A. M. Yaqub. Chicago, IL: The University of Chicago Press.

Ibn 'Adī, Yaḥyā (1988) 'Maqāla fī ghayr al-mutanāhī', in his *Maqālat Yaḥyā Ibn 'Adī al-falsafiyya*. Edited by S. Khalīfāt. Amman: University of Jordan Press, pp. 135–40.

Ibn Bājja (1991) *Sharḥ al-samā' al-ṭabī'ī li-Arasṭāṭālīs* [*Commentary on Aristotle's* Physics]. Edited by M. Fakhrī. Second Ed. Beirut: Dār al-nahār li-l-nashr.

Ibn Paquda, Bachya Ben Joseph (1996) *Duties of the Heart*. Translated into Hebrew by Ibn Tibbon and into English by Daniel Haberman. New York: Feldheim.

[Ibn Rushd] Averroes (1987) *Averroes' Tahafut al-Tahafut (The Incoherence of the Incoherence)*. Volumes I and II. Translated by S. Van Den Bergh. Cambridge: Cambridge University Press.

Ibn Rushd (1998) *Tahāfut al-Tahāfut* [*The Incoherence* of The Incoherence]. Edited by M. A. al-Jābirī. Beirut: Markaz al-dirasāt al-waḥda al-'arabiyya.

Ibn Sīnā (1959) *Al-Shifā', Al-Manṭiq, Al-Maqūlāt* [*The Categories* of The Healing]. Edited by J. Qanawātī, M. M. al-Khuḍayrī, A. F. al-Ihwānī, and S. Zāyid. Cairo: Al-Hay'a al-'āmma li-shu'ūn al-maṭābi' al-amīriyya.

Ibn Sīnā (1985) *Al-Najāt* [*The Salvation*]. Edited by M. T. Dānishpazhūh. Tehran: Tehran University Press.

[Ibn Sīnā] Avicenna (2009) *The Physics of the Healing*. Edited and translated by J. McGinnis. Provo, UT: Brigham Young University Press.

al-Khayyāt (1957) *Kitāb al-intiṣār wa-l-radd 'alā Ibn al-Rawandī al-mulḥid* [*The Book of Victory*]. Edited and translated into French by A. N. Nader. Beirut: Catholic Press.

al-Kindī (2012) *The Philosophical Works of al-Kindī*. Translated by P. Adamson and P. E. Pormann. Karachi: Oxford University Press.

Lucretius (2001) *On the Nature of Things*. Translated by M. F. Smith. Indianapolis, IN: Hackett.

Maimonides, Moses (1967) *The Guide of the Perplexed*. Translated by S. Pines. Chicago, IL: The University of Chicago Press.

Neckam, Alexandri (1863) *De Naturis Rerum* [*On the Nature of Things*]. Edited by T. Wright. London: Longman, Roberts, and Green.

Philoponus, John (2004) *Against Proclus on the Eternity of the World 1–5*. Translated by M. Share. London: Bloomsbury.

Philoponus, John (2014) *Against Aristotle on the Eternity of the World*. Translated by C. Wildberg. London: Bloomsbury.

Plutarch (1976) *Against the Stoics on Common Conceptions*, in *Moralia, Volume XIII: Part 2: Stoic Essays*. Edited and translated by H. Cherniss. Loeb Classical Library 470. Cambridge, MA: Harvard University Press.

al-Rāzī, Fakhr al-Dīn (1990) *Al-Mabāḥith al-mashriqiyya fī ʿilm al-ilāhiyyāt wa-l-ṭabīʿiyyāt* [*Eastern Investigations*]. Edited by M. al-Baghdādī. Two Vols. Beirut: Dār al-kitāb al-ʿarabī.

al-Rāzī, Fakhr al-Dīn (1994). *Sharḥ al-ʿuyūn al-ḥikma* [*Commentary on* Fountains of Wisdom]. Edited by M. Hejazi and A. A. Saqa. Tehran: Muʾassisa li-l-ṭabāʾa al-nashr.

al-Shahrastānī, Muḥammad (1846) *Kitab al-ilal wa al-niḥal: Books of Religions and Philosophical Sects*. Edited by W. Cureton. Two Vols. London: Society for the Publication of Oriental Texts.

al-Shahrastānī, Muḥammad (1934) *The Summa Philosophiae of al-Shahrastānī: Nihāyat al-iqdām fī ʿilm al-kalām* [*The End of Steps in Theology*]. Edited and translated by Alfred Guillaume. London: Oxford University Press.

al-Shahrastānī, Muḥammad (2001) *Struggling with the Philosopher: A Refutation of Avicenna's Metaphysics*. Edited and translated by T. Mayer, and W. Madelung. London: I.B.Tauris.

al-Suhrawardī, Shihāb al-Dīn (1999) *The Philosophy of Illumination*. Edited and translated by J. Walbridge, and H. Ziai. Provo, UT: Brigham Young University Press.

al-Tabrīzī, Muḥammad (1981) *Sharḥ-i bīst-u-panj muqqadama dar ithbāt-i bārī taʿālā* [*Commentary on the Twenty-Five Premises for the Proof of the Existence of God*]. Edited by M. Mohaghegh. Translated into Persian by S. J. Sajjadi. Tehran: The Institute of Islamic Studies (University of Tehran-McGill University).

al-Ṭūsī, Naṣīr al-Dīn (2004) *al-Maṣāriʿ al-Mūṣāriʿ* [*The Wrestlings Down of the Wrestler*]. Edited by W. Madelung. Tehran: The Institute of Islamic Studies (University of Tehran-McGill University).

William of Auvergne (1998) *The Universe of Creatures*. Selections Translated from the Latin with an Introduction and Notes by R. J. Teske. Milwaukee, WI: Marquette University Press.

Secondary References

Abdel Meguid, A. (2018) 'Al-Kindī's Argument for the Finitude of Time in His Critique of Aristotle's Theory of the Eternity of the World in the Treatise on First Philosophy: The Role of the Perceiving Soul and the Relation between Sensation and Intellection', *Journal of Islamic Studies*, 29(3), pp. 323–56.

Beşikci, M. N. (2022) 'Mehmed Emīn Üsküdārī's Sharḥ al-Barahīn al-khamsa on Infinity', *Nazariyat*, 8(1), pp. 101–43.

Beşikci, M. N. (forthcoming) 'A New Perspective on an Old Debate: Ismāʿīl Gelenbevī on Divine Knowledge and the Mapping Demonstration', in Qureshi, Y. (ed.) *An 18th-Century Ottoman Polymath: Ismāʿīl Gelenbevī*. Berlin: De Gruyter.

Bowin, J. (2007) 'Aristotelian Infinity', *Oxford Studies in Ancient Philosophy*, 32, pp. 233–50.

Brown, P. (1965) 'A Medieval Analysis of Infinity', *Journal of the History of Philosophy*, 3(2), pp. 242–43.

Busard, H. L. L. (1983) *The First Latin Translation of Euclid's Elements Commonly Ascribed to Adelard of Bath*. Toronto: Pontifical Institute of Medieval Studies.

Cohoe, C. (2013) 'There Must Be a First: Why Thomas Aquinas Rejects Infinite, Essentially Ordered, Causal Series', *British Journal for the History of Philosophy*, 21(5), pp. 838–56.

Coope, U. (2012) 'Aristotle on the Infinite', in Shield, C. (ed.), *The Oxford Handbook of Aristotle*. Oxford: Oxford University Press, pp. 267–86.

Cooper, J. (2016) 'Aristotelian Infinites', *Oxford Studies in Ancient Philosophy*, 51, pp. 161–206.

Craig, W. L. (1979) *The Kalām Cosmological Argument*. Basingstoke: Macmillan.

Davenport, A. (1999) *Measure of a Different Greatness: The Intensive Infinite, 1250–1650*. Leiden: Brill.

Davidson, H. A. (1969) 'John Philoponus as a Source of Medieval Islamic and Jewish Proofs of Creation', *Journal of the American Oriental Society*, 89(2), pp. 357–91.

Davidson, H. A. (1987) *Proofs for Eternity, Creation and the Existence of God in Medieval Islamic and Jewish Philosophy*. New York: Oxford University Press.

Dhanani, A. (1994) *The Physical Theory of Kalām*. Leiden: Brill.

Dhanani, A. (2015) 'The Impact of Ibn Sīnā's Critique of Atomism on Subsequent Kalām Discussions of Atomism', *Arabic Sciences and Philosophy*, 25(1), pp. 79–104.

Duhem, P. (1985) *Medieval Cosmology Theories of Infinity: Place, Time, Void, and the Plurality of Worlds*. Edited and translated by R. Ariew. Chicago: The University of Chicago Press.

Geach, P. T. (1967) 'Infinity in Scholastic Philosophy', in Lakatos, I. (ed.) *Problems in the Philosophy of Mathematics*. Amsterdam: North-Holland, pp. 41–42.

Grant, E. (ed.) (1974) *A Source Book in Medieval Science*. Cambridge, MA: Harvard University Press.

Gutas, D. (2014) *Avicenna and the Aristotelian Tradition*. Second Ed. Leiden: Brill.

Hintikka, J. (1966) 'Aristotelian Infinity', *The Philosophical Review*, 75(2), pp. 197–218.

Hodges, W. (2012) 'Affirmative and Negative in Ibn Sīnā', in Novaes, C. D., and Hjortland, O. T. (eds.) *Insolubles and Consequences: Essays in Honour of Stephen Read*. London: College Publications, pp. 119–34.

İskenderoğlu, M. (2002) *Fakhr-al-Dīn al-Rāzī and Thomas Aquinas on the Question of the Eternity of the World*. Leiden: Brill.

Kaukua, J. (2020) 'Avicenna on Negative Judgement', *Topoi*, 39(3), pp. 657–66.

Kohler, G. (2006) 'Medieval Infinities in Mathematics and the Contribution of Gersonides', *History of Philosophy Quarterly*, 23(2), pp. 95–116.

Kouremenos, T. (1995) *Aristotle on Mathematical Infinity*. Stuttgart: Franz Steiner Verlag.

Kretzmann, N. (1982) 'Syncategoremata, Sophismata, Exponibilia', in Kretzmann, N., Kenny, A., and Pinborg, J. (eds.) *Cambridge History of Later Medieval Philosophy*. Cambridge: Cambridge University Press, pp. 211–45.

Lammer, A. (2018) 'Two Sixth/Twelfth-Century Hardliners on Creation and Divine Eternity: al-Šahrastānī and Abū l-Barakāt al-Baġdādī on God's Priority over the World', in Al Ghouz, A. (ed.). *Islamic Philosophy from the 12th to the 14th Century*. Bonn: Bonn University Press.

Lear, J. (1980) 'Aristotelian Infinity', *Proceedings of the Aristotelian Society*, 80, pp. 187–210.

Mancosu, P. (2009) 'Measuring the Size of Infinite Collections of Natural Numbers: Was Cantor's Theory of Infinite Number Inevitable?', *The Review of Symbolic Logic*, 2(4), pp. 612–46.

Mancosu, P. (2016) *Abstraction and Infinity*. Oxford: Oxford University Press.

Mancosu, P. (forthcoming) *The Wilderness of Infinity: Robert Grosseteste, William of Auvergne and Mathematical Infinity in the Thirteenth Century*.

Marmura, M. E. (1960) 'Avicenna and the Problem of the Infinite Number of Souls', *Mediaeval Studies*, 22, 232–39.

Mayer, T. (2012) 'The Absurdities of Infinite Time: Shahrastānī's Critique of Ibn Sīnā and Ṭūṣī's Defence', in Hansberger, R., Afifi al-Akiti, M., and Burnett, C. (eds.) *Medieval Arabic Thought: Essays in Honour of Fritz Zimmermann*. London: The Warburg Institute, pp. 103–34.

McGinnis, J. (2010). 'Avicennan Infinity: A Select History of the Infinite through Avicenna', *Documenti e studi sulla tradizione filosofica medievale*, 21, pp. 199–221.

McGinnis, J. (2014). 'The Eternity of the World: Proofs and Problems in Aristotle, Avicenna, and Aquinas', *American Catholic Philosophical Quarterly*, 88(2), pp. 271–88.

Monnot, G. (1996) 'Al-Shahrastānī', in Fleet, K., Krämer, G., Matringe, D, Nawas, J., and Rowson, E. (eds.) *Encyclopedia of Islam*. Brill: Leiden, pp. 214–16.

Moore, A. W. (2019) *The Infinite*. Third Ed. New York: Routledge.

Murdoch, J. E. (1964) 'Superposition, Congruence and Continuity in the Middle Ages', in Cohen, I. B., and Taton, R. (eds.) *Mélanges Alexandre Koyré I: L'Aventure de la Science*. Paris: Hermann, pp. 416–41.

Murdoch, J. E. (1968) 'The Equality of Infinites in the Middle Ages', *Actes du XI congrès international d'histoire des sciences*, vol. III. Paris, pp. 171–74.

Murdoch, J. E. (1969) 'Mathesis in Philosophiam Scholasticam Introducta: The Rise and Development of the Application of Mathematics in Fourteenth Century Philosophy and Theology', in *Arts libéraux et philosophie au moyen âge, Actes du IVe congrés international de philosophie médiévale.* Montréal: Librairie philosophique J. Vrin, pp. 215–56.

Murdoch, J. E. (1981) 'Mathematics and Infinity in the Later Middle Ages', *Proceedings of the American Catholic Philosophical Association*, 55, pp. 40–58.

Murdoch, J. E. (1982) 'Infinity and Continuity', in Kretzmann, N., Kenny, A., and Pinborg, J. (eds.) *The Cambridge History of Later Medieval Philosophy.* Cambridge: Cambridge University Press, pp. 564–91.

Nawar, T. (2015) 'Aristotelian Finitism', *Synthese*, 192(8), pp. 2345–60.

Pines, S. (1972) 'An Arabic Summary of a Lost Work of John Philoponus', *Israel Oriental Studies*, 2 pp. 320–52 (repr. in Pines, S. (1986) *Studies in Arabic Versions of Greek Texts and in Medieval* Science. Leiden: Brill, pp. 294–326).

Pines, S. (1997) *Studies in Islamic Atomism*. Translated by S. Schwarz and edited by T. Langermann. Jerusalem: The Magnes Press.

Reck, E. (2023) 'Dedekind's Contributions to the Foundations of Mathematics', in Zalta, E. N., and Nodelman, U. (eds.) *The Stanford Encyclopedia of Philosophy* (Winter 2023 Edition). https://plato.stanford.edu/archives/win2023/entries/dedekind-foundations/.

Rescher, N., and Khatchadourian, H. (1965) 'Al-Kindī's Epistle on the Finitude of the Universe'. *Isis* 56(4), pp. 426–33.

Rioux, J. W. (2023) *Thomas Aquinas' Mathematical Realism*. Cham: Palgrave Macmillan.

Russell, B. (2010 [1903]) *Principles of Mathematics*. New York: Routledge.

Shamsi, F. A. (1975) 'Epistle on What Cannot Be Infinite and of What Infinity May Be Attributed', *Islamic Studies*, 14(2), pp. 123–44.

Shihadeh, A. (2011) 'Khojazāda on al-Ghazālī's Criticism of the Philosophers' Proof of the Existence of God' in Yücedoğru, T., Koloğlu, O. Ş., Kılavuz, U. M., and Gömbeyaz, K. (eds.) *International Symposium on Khojazāda*. Bursa: Bursa Metropolitan Municipality, pp. 141–60.

Sider, T. (2007) 'Parthood', *The Philosophical Review*, 116(1), pp. 51–91.

Studtmann, P. (2004) 'Aristotle's Category of Quantity: A Unified Interpretation', *Apeiron*, 37(1), pp. 69–91.

Świętorzecka, K., Pietruszczak, A., and Zarepour, M. S. (forthcoming) 'A Formal Reconstruction of Avicenna's Proof of the Sincere'.

Sylla, E. D. (2021) 'Infinity and Continuity Thomas Bradwardine and His Contemporaries', in Shapiro, S., and Hellman, G. (eds.) *The History of Continua: Philosophical and Mathematical Perspectives*. Oxford: Oxford University Press, pp. 49–81.

Teske, R. J. (1990) 'William of Auvergne on the Eternity of the World', *The Modern Schoolman*, 67(3), pp. 187–205.

Teske, R. J. (1995) 'William of Auvergne's Arguments for the Newness of the World', *Mediaevalia: Textos e Estudos*, 7–8, pp. 287–302.

Teske, R. J. (2000) 'William of Auvergne on Time and Eternity', *Traditio*, 55, pp. 125–41.

Thom, P. (2008) 'Al-Fārābī on Indefinite and Privative Names', *Arabic Sciences and Philosophy*, 18(2), pp. 193–209.

Uckelman, S. L. (2015) 'The Logic of Categorematic and Syncategorematic Infinity', *Synthese*, 192(8), pp. 2361–77.

van Ess, J. (2017). *Theology and Society in the Second and Third Centuries of the Hijra*. Translated by G. Goldbloom. Vol. 2. Leiden: Brill.

Wolfson, H. A. (1929) *Crescas' Critique of Aristotle*. Cambridge, MA: Harvard University Press.

Zarepour, M. S. (2016) 'Avicenna on the Nature of Mathematical Objects', *Dialogue*, 55(3), pp. 511–36.

Zarepour, M. S. (2020) 'Avicenna on Mathematical Infinity', *Archiv für Geschichte der Philosophie*, 102(3), pp. 379–425.

Zarepour, M. S. (2022a) 'Arabic and Islamic Philosophy of Mathematics', in Zalta, E. N., and Nodelman, U. (eds.) *The Stanford Encyclopedia of Philosophy* (Summer 2022 Edition). https://plato.stanford.edu/archives/sum2022/entries/arabic-islamic-phil-math/.

Zarepour, M. S. (2022b) *Necessary Existence and Monotheism*. Cambridge: Cambridge University Press.

Zarepour, M. S. (forthcoming) 'The Evolution of the Mapping Argument in Avicenna's Oeuvre'.

Acknowledgements

I owe a deep debt of gratitude to my wife, Samaneh, for her constant encouragement and love, without which I doubt I would have found the drive and focus to pursue this project and probably many of my other projects.

I should also thank Amal Awad, Necmeddin Beşikci, Gholamreza Dadkhah, Andreas Lammer, Fraser MacBride, Paolo Mancosu, Jon McGinnis, and Tony Street for stimulating discussions on ideas presented in this Element. I am particularly indebted to Paolo Mancosu and Necmeddin Beşikci for generously sharing copies of their forthcoming works. My thanks also extend to Kaave Lajevardi and two anonymous reviewers for their valuable feedback on an earlier draft of this Element. This work would have never seen the light of day without the patience and support of Stewart Shapiro, to whom I would like to express my gratitude. I am grateful to the Leverhulme Trust for awarding me a 2023 Philip Leverhulme Prize, which provided crucial support during the final stages of this project. *Wal-ḥamdu li-l-lāhi awwalan wa ākhirā*.

I want to dedicate this Element to my daughter, Sophia, who is a finitist by the force of age! She can count only to ten and does not yet know anything about infinity. Nevertheless, she knows how to make her father infinitely happy.

Cambridge Elements

The Philosophy of Mathematics

Penelope Rush
University of Tasmania

From the time Penny Rush completed her thesis in the philosophy of mathematics (2005), she has worked continuously on themes around the realism/anti-realism divide and the nature of mathematics. Her edited collection, *The Metaphysics of Logic* (Cambridge University Press, 2014), and forthcoming essay 'Metaphysical Optimism' (*Philosophy Supplement*), highlight a particular interest in the idea of reality itself and curiosity and respect as important philosophical methodologies.

Stewart Shapiro
The Ohio State University

Stewart Shapiro is the O'Donnell Professor of Philosophy at The Ohio State University, a Distinguished Visiting Professor at the University of Connecticut, and Professorial Fellow at the University of Oslo. His major works include *Foundations without Foundationalism* (1991), *Philosophy of Mathematics: Structure and Ontology* (1997), *Vagueness in Context* (2006), and *Varieties of Logic* (2014). He has taught courses in logic, philosophy of mathematics, metaphysics, epistemology, philosophy of religion, Jewish philosophy, social and political philosophy, and medical ethics.

About the Series

This Cambridge Elements series provides an extensive overview of the philosophy of mathematics in its many and varied forms. Distinguished authors will provide an up-to-date summary of the results of current research in their fields and give their own take on what they believe are the most significant debates influencing research, drawing original conclusions.

Cambridge Elements

The Philosophy of Mathematics

Elements in the Series

Number Concepts: An Interdisciplinary Inquiry
Richard Samuels and Eric Snyder

The Euclidean Programme
A. C. Paseau and Wesley Wrigley

Mathematical Rigour and Informal Proof
Fenner Stanley Tanswell

Mathematical Pluralism
Graham Priest

The Mereology of Classes
Gabriel Uzquiano

Iterative Conceptions of Set
Neil Barton

Introducing the Philosophy of Mathematical Practice
Jessica Carter

Mathematics is (mostly) Analytic
Gregory Lavers

Mathematical Notations
Dirk Schlimm

Elements of Purity
Andrew Arana

Husserl's Philosophy of Mathematical Practice
Mirja Hartimo

Medieval Finitism
Mohammad Saleh Zarepour

A full series listing is available at: www.cambridge.org/EPM

Printed in the United States
by Baker & Taylor Publisher Services